Troubled Kids Need Jesus Too

By
Larry D. Veal

Copyright 2021 © Larry D. Veal
ISBN 978-1-68564-182-5

This book is designed to provide accurate and authoritative information regarding the subject matter covered. This information is given with the understanding that neither the author nor LEEDS PRESS CORP is engaged in rendering legal or professional advice. The opinions expressed by the author are not necessarily those of LEEDS PRESS CORP

Copyright 2021 © Leeds Press Corp

Cover copyright 2021 © Leeds Press Corp

Cover Design by Leeds Graphics.

Editorial by Leeds Press Corp

Written by Larry D. Veal

Leeds Press Corp encourages the right to free expression and the importance of copyright. The objective of copyright is to encourage authors and artists to produce the innovative works that strengthens our society. Troubled Kids Need Jesus Too - No part of this publication may be reproduced, stored in a retrieval system, or transmitted in any way by any means, electronic, mechanical, photocopy, recording or otherwise without the prior permission of the author except as provided by USA copyright law. If you would like permission to use material from the book (other than for review purposes), please contact info@leedspress.com. The opinions expressed by the author are not necessarily those of LEEDS PRESS CORP.

Leedspublishing.com

Twitter.com/ Leedspresscorp

Instagram.com/ Leedspresscorp

Facebook.com/ Leedspresscorp

LP BOOKS is an imprint of LEEDS PRESS CORP. Name and Logo is a trademark of LEEDS PRESS CORP. The publisher is not responsible for websites (or their content) that are not owned by the publisher.

LEEDS PRESS SPEAKERS AGENCY provides a wide range of authors for speaking events. To find out more; info@leedspress.com or call 323-230-0062

Printed in the United States of America.

Copyright 2021 © Larry D. Veal

Troubled Kids Need Jesus Too

By
Larry D. Veal

Contents

FOREWORD	7
SECTION ONE	10
"Discovering Self"	10
CHAPTER ONE	11
Knuckle-Head	11
CHAPTER TWO	19
Like an Elephant on a Chicken Farm	19
CHAPTER THREE	26
Our Gang	26
CHAPTER FOUR	32
Dumb Fools	32
CHAPTER FIVE	35
No Little Rascals	35
CHAPTER SIX	43
Cultural Differences	43
CHAPTER SEVEN	48
Winds Of Change	48
SECTION TWO	57
"Discovering God"	57
CHAPTER EIGHT	58
Looking For Strength	58
CHAPTER NINE	64
The Testimony	64
CHAPTER TEN	70
The Fight	70
CHAPTER ELEVEN	74
Faith	74
A Change In High Schools	79

SECTION III	83
"Moving In the Spirit"	83
CHAPTER TWELVE	84
Through Faith in Jesus	84
CHAPTER THIRTEEN	91
Being Rewarded for Doing The Right Thing	91
CHAPTER FOURTEEN	97
The Best Mental Attitude Award	97
CHAPTER FIFTEEN	104
God's Voice	104
CHAPTER SIXTEEN	113
Like a Thief, a Thief, a Thief in The Night	113
CHAPTER SEVENTEEN	132
The Blueprint	132
CHAPTER EIGHTTEEN	136
A Vow to Keep	136
CHAPTER NINETEEN	140
Let's Serve	140
CHAPTER TWENTY	145
Decisions	145
CHAPTER TWENTY-ONE	147
Godly Intentions	147
ABOUT THE AUTHOR	149

LARRY D. VEAL

FOREWORD

"I think Jesus would be proud" stated Rapper Snoop Doggie Dog. This statement was made in an interview that the rapper had with writer Rych McCain in the Florida Star Newspaper issued on May 29, 2004. Snoop was asked the question about how he felt Jesus would feel if He heard the explicit language in one of his songs. Snoop went on to give a very thought provoking answer " …Jesus loves us. He don't hate nothing about us no matter what we do." To know that Snoop seeks to understand the depth of Jesus' love is an awesome revelation, and to be concern that Jesus considers us regardless of what we do is also great. However, to know that Jesus' love is what he gives to us is one thing, but to understand that we also must give back to Him is something else. Young people understand that Jesus loves them regardless of where they are from, or what they do, they understand this for the most part. But one thing that is not so clear is what am I supposed to do for Him, how am I supposed to give back to Him, especially when I am living in a world that may not honor that, a world that may not show someone like me how to exist: truly exist, the way Jesus would like for me to?

In writing this book it was my revelation that many troubled youth want to live better for God. They don't care to struggle with the lies, fights, drugs, and anger that exist in their environment. However, many are not being taught. This statement was reiterated in this article with Snoop, he went on to say"so by mentioning Him (Jesus), says that we are open to be taught, to learn, to do the right things. But how many older people are coming down teaching us and educating us? Who is giving classes, whose looking out for us? "But you want to fault us and blame us when we say what we say. Where are our fathers at? Where are our grandfathers? Where you mother$#@&* at that's talking all this %$#@? Come down and help us instead of criticizing us."

This sentiment is the absolute basis for this book. It will show the reader the importance of knowing why it is imperative to live a life that honors Jesus. It will not teach scripture, by scripture interpretation nor is it intended to preach. This book is designed to show the troubled young man or woman the quiet peace that God will give you even in your trouble. Also, it will hopefully encourage the adults, especially the ones who are looking at the troubles that our children are having as if there is no hope, to play an active role in their lives. In many cases all that is needed is for some of us, so-called Spirit-filled individuals to teach a child or encourage them on the importance of living right. Showing them how to follow the life of the ultimate instructor Jesus Christ. Snoop went on to say" And what I am doing is expressing me because this is all I know. If I was taught something differently, hey I would. But since you #@%&%$ are sittin up there and aint teaching us, crap forget ya"ll, I am doing it my way!"

In this story Jeffrey learns, through his trials as a child, and adolescence the importance of accepting Jesus' words. It is fortunate that through his troubles, his thievery, fights, racist thoughts, and anger, he learns the importance of Jesus' love for him and understands the true meaning behind "Troubled Kids Need Jesus Too"

"Not only can you not tell a book by its cover, you also cannot tell it by the first couple of Chapters." This was said as a part of a speech by the valedictorian of a Florida high school. This student spent his first year of high school in jail.

SECTION ONE
"Discovering Self"

CHAPTER ONE
Knuckle-Head

All I could think about while I sat on the back seat of the 17th and College Avenue city bus going to Glendale Mall was that doggone bike seat. I had to have it. You see, most people in my neighborhood couldn't afford a new bike, so we would find bits and pieces and put them together. Most of us guys would start with a bike frame that we'd go to the junk yard and steal. This time, I had a real good one. It was all put together, except for the seat. I didn't want just any seat. I wanted a good one.

As the bus rolled into the parking lot of the mall, I began searching the area. I got off and started walking across the parking lot, with my wire cutters in my pants, daydreaming about that seat, when all of a sudden; a car's horn blew.

"Get out of the way, you little coon!" a white man yelled from the car.

The man then got out of his car and started to walk angrily towards me. I began to run, when a tall black man, who had seen everything through the mall's glass doors, came exiting.

"Don't run little brother," he said.

I then facetiously responded, "I wasn't. I ain't scared of that stupid honkey."

The white man then retreated to his automobile as me and the black stranger laughed and went our separate ways.

I was only at the mall for about fifteen minutes before I saw the bike seat of my dreams. It was trimmed in chrome, and it was high in the back.

"Oh yeah," I said. "That bike seat is mine."

I looked around the parking lot and didn't see anyone. I approached the bike and kneeled in order to begin my operation. As I was trying to remove the seat, I had more trouble than I anticipated. I looked around the lot again. This time I saw a police car way on the other side of the parking lot. No need to be alarmed. I know he didn't see me. I continued struggling to remove the seat. It was finally coming off when I looked down and saw some black shiny shoes. I slowly followed the shoes on up to the face.

Oh no! It was a policewoman.

For some reason, even though I was surprised, I wasn't scared. Shoot, I'm from the 'hood. Either way it goes, I'm not going to let no weak, generic policewoman take me to jail.

The woman looked at me like a mother who caught her child's hand in the cookie jar. "What are you doing?" she asked.

"I'm just takin' off this seat to my bike, ma'am, because I'm tired of leavin' my bike here, and comin' back to it with either the seat or the wheels gone. I don't understand it. You would think that with all of these police around, my bike would be safe. I'll tell you what, ma'am, Officer Friendly. All I came to do was get somethin' for my mother. Could you please watch my bike while I'm gone? I promise to come right back."

"Well, son, I can't just sit here and watch your bike. There are a lot of things I have to do," she said sympathetically.

Yes! I'm fooling this dumb lady.

"Well, ma'am, since you know it's my bike, please stop anybody else from botherin' it, if you happen to see them while I'm gone."

"Okay. I'll do what I can," she said.

"Thanks." I then ran into the mall and hauled butt over to the other side to catch the bus back home.

As I sat on the bus I was thinking. Damn! I'm a smart twelve year-old, even though I still didn't get my freakin' bike seat.

When I returned home, I saw some of the fellas playing basketball in the alley behind Big Boo's house. Boo was a little older than I was, but he was much bigger. He didn't fight much, but I've seen him kick people's butts if they made him mad.

The guys were playing a game of twenty-one. I decided to join them. All during the game, people were just pushing, shoving, cursing, and scratching. In other words, we were playing ball as usual. However, this time things were a little different for me because Big Boo and I kept pushing and yelling at each other. That usually didn't happen because we were pretty cool with one another.

The way we'd play the game is like this. The two people with the lowest scores at the end of each game had to leave the game. Big Boo and I were the last two left in this game, and, we both wanted to win. He obviously wanted to win more than I did, because he kept pushing me down. I was getting ticked off, and I told him if he did it again, I was gonna kick his butt. I didn't care how big he was.

It was always like that with me. Whenever, I fight someone, the other person is usually bigger than me. I guess you could say I liked a challenge. Anyway, Boo and I kept playing ball, and guess what?

He pushed me down again. This time, I got up and hit him in the face causing him to fall down. When he got up, he began to charge towards me. By then, I had reached into my pocket and pulled out a switchblade.

"Come on, punk. What you gon' do?" I said.

He stood there looking stupid, because he knew I'd cut his big goofy butt into at least four pieces. I knew he was very scared because of the look on his face. I love that look. I like making people scared and weak.

By that time a crowd had gathered. I liked crowds. So, I guess I'll exaggerate this a little bit. I walked over to Big Boo and grabbed him by his neck. I put him in a headlock and started threatening him.

"I told you to stop messin' with me, didn't I? But, you don't wanna listen. Do you give up?"

He didn't respond. By then, tears started coming out of his eyes. I heard one of my friends yell from the crowd, "Here comes his Momma!"

I looked around and sho 'nuff, his big ugly Momma was jogging up to where we were. She was just cussing up a storm. She was telling me to let him go and that she had called the police. I knew she must have called the cops, because I heard a siren in the distance.

"You lucky your Momma's comin', punk," I said. Then I ran over to a dilapidated house to get rid of the knife.

They all saw me put the knife in my sock before I ran. So, I knew they'd tell the police that. Therefore, I decided to play the smart role. I threw the knife away, then put an old stick where the knife was. I did that so that when the police come, they'll search me and all they'll find is a stick. I'll tell them that was what I had all along. You see, I had to do it that way, because if I just left the scene, they'd have probable cause to come and pick me up.

I then went back to the scene of the crime. By the time I got there, the police were just pulling up. They came from both ends of the alley. Before one policeman could get out of the car, Boo's fat Momma ran over there and damn near knocked him down.

"He tried to kill my baby," she said angrily as she pointed to me. "He pulled a knife out and had it to his neck. Take him away, officer, he don't belong 'round here."

The policemen approached me and asked if I had a knife. I told then no. They then made me spread eagle on the police car. One big black officer with an afro said, as he began to pat me down, "I hope you got a knife, 'cause I'm gonna like throwing your little butt in jail."

The officer started patting my shoulders and worked his way down to my feet. By the time he got to my socks, he felt the stick. Before he could pull it out, he said, "Hell, yeah. I got your little behind now. I'm takin' you down."

"Oh, yeah? When did people start getting arrested for carrying little sticks around, officer?" I asked him.

The officer pulled the object completely out of my sock and stared at it like he was very disappointed.

"That ain't what he had," yelled Big Boo's Momma.

"Yeah, that ain't what he had," added Boo. "That buster had a knife, didn't hey'all?"

I don't know why he asked anybody. He knew that they wouldn't tell on me. At that time the officers pulled Boo and his mother to the side and began talking to them. I wasn't worried at all. I was too smart for all of those weak knuckleheads.

The officers had been talking to them for about twenty minutes, when all of a sudden, my mother came out of nowhere.

"What's goin' on, boy? What you done did now?" she asked angrily.

The officers approached my mother and explained what was happening. When they were finished, she turned and looked at me as if she knew I was guilty. Before I could tell her that I hadn't done anything she said, "Shut up. You bet' not say nothin.'"

After that, the officers just told my mother to take me home and that if I came around Boo's house again; they'd take me to juvenile hall. On the way home my mother was squeezing my neck. My little sister, Pat, was just laughing away talking about, "You so bad. Momma, you need to whip him."

"Shut up, gal," my mother replied.

However, when I got home, I did get a whipping. But I got them so much that I was immune to them. There were times when I got spankings two and three times a day for doing different things. I don't know where my mother got the energy.

Out of all my mother's seven children, I was the one who got in the most trouble.

A lot of people used to tease me by telling me that I was adopted. But I knew that it wasn't true, because if I were adopted, they would've given me back by now. Plus, I looked just like my grandfather. He was the most handsome man I'd ever seen.

We lived in a small three-bedroom, one story house. Altogether, there were twelve of us living there-- my mother, my brothers and sisters, and my uncles and aunts that my mother brought from Mississippi when my grandmother died. Everyone in our neighborhood knew I had a big family. I guess that's one reason why I got away with so much mischief. Sometimes when I'd get in trouble, my mother would have my oldest brothers, June and Jerry, hold me down while she whipped me. Other times, she'd just put me on a stay at home punishment. However, she stopped doing that because I'd always crawl out of the window and go somewhere anyway.

Once when I crawled out of the window, I went over to my friend, Curtis' house. While over there, his uncle came in and asked us if we wanted to make some money. Of course, we said yes without even finding out how. He said he had a job he wanted us to do.

I assumed that Curtis' uncle was about twenty two. Anyway, he said that he saw a car parked down the street with its doors unlocked. In the back seat was a box with a bunch of brand new hair care products in it. He guessed the guy was a beautician. At any rate, he wanted us to go and steal the box from the car and bring it to him. Immediately I agreed. It was too simple. But I had to convince Curtis to do it. I told him that all he had to do was be the lookout and I'd do the rest. Curtis agreed.

When we got to the corner, there was the car. We saw the box and the unlocked doors. I cautiously opened the door, removed the box, and hurriedly took it back to Curtis' uncle. "That was a piece of cake," I said.

Curtis was very nervous. He was looking out of the window trying to see if the police were coming. His uncle and I laughed at him. His uncle then gave each of us a dollar and thanked us for a job well done.

I was satisfied with the dollar. After all, it was more than I had, and, it was a simple task. I didn't think about that incident again until years later. It was then that I thought about the fact that we could've easily been shot for that.

CHAPTER TWO
Like an Elephant on a Chicken Farm

A lot of times when Curtis and I and some more of the fellas would get tired of hanging in the 'hood, we'd try to think of someplace else to go. Most of the time that would be to the malls or downtown. My mother told me never to go downtown without her knowing. But you know how that goes.

This particular day I ran into Bobby while he was riding his bike down Carrollton Avenue. To me, Bobby was what I would call a rich kid. They weren't really rich. They actually lived in a small one-bedroom apartment. But Bobby was an only child.

Therefore, he'd usually get what he wanted. Whenever Bobby and I would get together, it would be when I ran into him on the street. His mother and father didn't allow me around their house. They forbade him to hang out with me.

"What's up, Bob? What you gettin' into, brother?" I said. "Nothing, man. I'm just trying to stay out of trouble." "What for?" I asked. "Ain't no fun if it ain't no trouble."

I must have been talking to Bob for about ten minutes before I spotted this skinny gold pin he had on. It was pinned to his shirt the letter "B." Those pins were in style. A lot of people had them, but I never thought about getting one until I saw his.

"I like that gold pin, man. Where did you get it?"

"My mother bought it for me last week from J.C. Penney for my thirteenth birthday," he said.

"Man, I got to get me one of those. That's sharp."

Bobby told me that the pin was expensive because it was real gold. What did I care if it was expensive? What did that mean? If I said I wanted it, I was gonna get it.

I can't remember paying for too many things anyway. Why should I pay for something? I was a master thief. I'm serious. This might sound crazy, but sometimes I felt God put me on this earth to steal. I used to steal so much that one time I stole something and started to go to the cashier to ask her for a receipt.

Anyway, I had to have that sharp-looking pin that Bobby had. So, one day I caught the Metro bus downtown to J.C. Penney. I went inside the store and roamed around for about thirty minutes. I used to do that in order to scope the place out. You know, look for the hidden cameras and look for suspicious looking people who would usually be undercover security guards.

I thought those guards were so funny. They'd try to be undercover, but, to me, they stood out like an elephant on a chicken farm. Sometimes they would be the only ones in the store with shades on, or the only ones with trench coats on in the summertime. I was so confident in my ability to steal that I could be the only customer in the store with those guys on all sides of me, and I knew I could still take something without them seeing me.

Well, now I'm approaching the jewelry section. Good. There are those gold pins. I looked at all the ones they had there. They had some with your full name. I didn't want that goofy lookin' stuff. I wanted a"J."

Well, what do you know? There it is, just as shiny as ever. That's mine. They may as well make it easy on themselves and hand it over to me.

As I looked at the pin, I also looked around to see if anyone was watching. I didn't see anybody, so now it's time to do what I came here for. In order to play it off, I picked up two pins with the letter "J" on them. However, I only put one back. The other, I slid into my left rear pocket as I pulled my wallet out. I looked in my wallet to make it seem as though I was looking for money to pay for something. After hanging out at that counter for a little while longer, I placed the wallet back in my pocket.

Before leaving the store, I walked around for about five more minutes. At that time, I headed towards the exit door. This is the scariest part of it all. Any minute, someone could grab you and say, "You're under arrest." I'm not afraid of getting arrested. I just don't want to get embarrassed like that.

I finally reached the set of interior doors. As I headed towards the set of exterior doors, I noticed a lady standing there. She was looking straight in my eyes. She then approached me. I could see her coming from the corner of my eyes. It kinda looked like she was coming in slow motion. Then I realized she was a cop.

"Excuse me, young man," she said. Then she pulled out a badge. "My name is...I'm with the store security. We observed that you picked up a gold pin and didn't put it back."

back." I'm a good actor so I knew it was time for me to play a role.

"What are you talkin' about? I put that pin back," I said with tears in my eyes. "No, you didn't put it back. You picked up two of them and you only put one.

At that point I knew I had to think fast, 'cause like I said, I'm too smart to let these phony police people catch me stealing.

"No, ma'am, I put both of the pins back."

I then placed my left hand in my back pocket as if to be just getting casual. As I was pulling my hand out of my pocket, I was also pulling the pin out. I didn't stop talking to the security lady while I was doing this. In fact, I was making a lot of facial expressions and gestures with my right hand. As the pin got halfway out of my pocket, I began to speak louder and to motion more. What I wanted to do was to drop the pin on the floor without her noticing it. Well, here it goes. The pin was falling towards the floor. I pulled my hand completely out of my pocket and took one step towards her, so that she could focus more on me. My voice got louder as the pin hit the floor. Well, I'll be. She didn't notice it. I then took one step back in order to place my left foot over the pin.

Now it's all done. I felt more comfortable now, because the pin was not on my person but on the floor with my foot over it.

"You're going to have to come downstairs with me, young man. We have to search you before I can let you go," she said.

"Fine. It don't matter to me 'cause I told you I ain't got no pin."

As I began to take a step to go with her, I smoothly kicked the pin in the corner of the exit door. When I got downstairs with her, there was a white man down there too. He was looking like Colombo on drugs or something.

"Pull your pants down, young man, and, turn your pockets inside out," Colombo said.

I did what he asked, but all the while I was telling them that I was no thief and that this was a big mistake. After they looked inside my shoes and everything, they said I could go. The lady then apologized. I told her not to worry about it and that I understood that there were a lot of people who were stealing merchandise and that they had to be careful. The lady shook my hand and encouraged me to do the right things. I told her I would and walked back upstairs.

As I was leaving the store, I strolled toward the area where the pin was. There I kneeled down, as if to tie up my shoe, then I picked the pin up and put it in my shoe and walked out of the store. That's right. I'm bad. I hate to toot my own horn, but I'm a bad boy.

When I returned home, I saw Bob riding his bike in the middle of the street doing wheelies.

"Yo, Bobby! Come here!" I yelled. Bobby stopped doing wheelies and came over to me.

"Yeah, what it be like?" he said.

"Well, you see somethin' different." I was wearing a faded Indiana Pacers hat. At that time, the Pacers were one of the best teams in the ABA. The pin was in the middle of the hat.

"You thief," he said surprisingly. "You don' got a pin. How'd you get that?" I explained how I got the pin.

"I don't know how you do it, but you always gettin' away with somethin' like that."

Bobby used to admire the way I would steal. He said I made it look easy. A while back when Bobby and I were at Indiana Square Mall, I stole something out of this Chinese clothing store. That day, Bobby told me that if I'd do it, he'd do it. Well, I never backed down from a challenge. Therefore, I went into the store. Bobby was waiting for me out in the hall, because I didn't care to steal while people were with me. I always felt that no one was as smooth as I was, and I wasn't getting caught for someone else's mistake.

I was in the store for about thirty minutes. When I came out, there was Bobby, waiting patiently.

"What took you so long, man?" he asked.

"Shoot, that was hard, man. Those Chinese people stick to you like glue." "Well, did you get something?"

"Do you see anything different?"

He checked me out from head to toe.

"You little thug. You stole those shoes," he said out loud.

"Be quiet! People might hear you, stupid." What I did was, put on a pair of their new shoes and placed my old ones in their shoebox. That was one of the oldest tricks in the book, but it still worked sometimes.

Bobby was just staring at my shoes with this look of fascination in his eyes. "I'm gonna get me some of those," he said.

I really didn't want him to go back in the store, because I was afraid that by now, they might have found my old shoes and thus, be on the alert. I could tell that it didn't matter what I said, Bobby was going to go back and get him some shoes, regardless.

As Bobby entered the store, I stood on the other side of the mall and watched him.

I was laughing at him already; 'cause he even walked into the store like he was gonna steal something. He had a real goofy walk anyway. He would walk on the tip of his toes and bounce whenever he stepped.

Bobby had been in the store for about forty minutes, when all of a sudden I heard someone yell from the store, "Hey! Hey! You come back here!"

Then all I saw was Bobby running out of the store with a frightened look on his face. And guess what, y'all? The fool had the whole box of shoes in his hand. I don't know what he was thinking about. All I knew was that little Chinese man started chasing him up and down the mall. Then some uniformed security guards joined in the chase.

They pursued him around the corner out of my view. I started walking down their way to see if he'd gotten away. But, before I could make it all the way there, the security guards were escorting Bobby back around the corner towards the store. He had on handcuffs and his hair was messed up. It looked as though he gave them a struggle. Behind them came the little Chinese man. He was breathing hard and mumbling some Chinese words.

It bothered me that my buddy got caught stealing. Even though it was a serious matter, I couldn't help but laugh as I was riding on the bus back home. I must admit, it did look funny. The next day I found out that Bobby didn't go to jail. His mother and father were advised of the situation, and they went to pick him up from the mall. After the incident, Bobby didn't want to hear anything about stealing. He didn't even want you to mention Chinese people any more. In fact, Bobby was so afraid of them after that; he stopped going to Bruce Lee movies. I teased him about that a lot. Once I put some chopsticks in his school lunch box. He was furious.

CHAPTER THREE
Our Gang

Most of the kids in our neighborhood went to School #61. It was a public school across from the Indianapolis 500 racetrack. If we were good, the teachers would reward us by taking us over to the track at least twice a year to see the drivers qualify. To this day I've never seen any drivers qualify.

I had been attending School #61 for three years. We were transferred there from a school that was much closer to our homes. School #61 was predominately white. It used to be all white until we got there, so you know that we weren't received well.

I used to get in trouble basically every day at school. I quickly became a well-known troublemaker to all the kids and teachers. When I was in the fifth grade, I would do disgusting things for no reason. I remember when I brought a bunch of roaches and ants to school and let them loose in class. All the kids were screaming and standing on tables. Even the teacher, Mrs. Garrison, was screaming. That was so funny.

That same year I got in trouble for hitting the music teacher in the face. She saw me pass candy to my friend. Then she told me to give it to her. I said no and put the candy in my pocket. She ordered me to give her the candy. She reached in my pocket to get it. It was then that I hit her in the face with my fist. I must have hit that old lady hard because she began to panic and told somebody to get Mr. Hayes, the school principal.

Mr. Jack Hayes knew me well. I don't know who used to whip me more, him or my mother.

Anyway, I was suspended from school for hitting that old lady. I remember that well. It happened two days before spring break. As a result of that, my mother made me stay in the house all week long. It was difficult for me to sneak out of the house these days. The rest of my family was on break too, and they kept an eye on me to make sure I didn't go anywhere.

Since I had to stay in the house, all I did was watch TV. There was this one particular movie I saw that stuck with me. It was a movie about gangs. The star of the movie was Pat Boone. I don't remember the name, but I do remember the details. Pat Boone played the role of a preacher who was concerned with ending the gang warfare on this troubled side of town. Throughout the movie, Pat Boone would try to encourage the gangs to get along. He'd quote biblical scriptures and use biblical reasons to get the groups to see eye to eye. After all of his unsuccessful attempts, he finally got them all to agree to meet up in one place. Once they arrived at this designated area, they agreed to listen to him. He gave a sermon on unity. After his sermon, he distributed little Bibles. Not knowing if he reached the guys yet, he asked if everything was now okay. One young gang member stood up and said, "No, everything isn't okay."

Pat Boone then said, with a look of disappointment, thinking that he had failed, "What is the problem? Why is everything not okay?"

The young member replied, "This Bible is too small. I can hardly read the words."

Almost in unison, the other gang members from both sides agreed that the Bibles were too small. With a look of great satisfaction and relief, Pat Boone then enthusiastically distributed larger Bibles to everyone. At least that's how I remember it. For some reason that movie stayed with me more than any other movie that I had seen during that time.

The most serious gang in our neighborhood during that time was the 24th Street Mad Dogs, the Baby Gangsters and the Black Cobras. They all liked to hurt and rob people. They rarely invaded each other's territory, but when they did, look out!

Most of the trouble that I got into during that time, I got into by myself. I would sometimes have one or two more people with me, but that was unusual. It wasn't until the seventh grade that I decided to join a gang. It was a gang with mostly neighborhood kids in it. Even though the gang was comprised of a whole lot of guys, there were only about seven of us who used to hang tough. We couldn't really trust the other guys, but we knew that as long as we all were together, if one person fought, we all fought.

Many times, while we were in the neighborhood, we would fight other gangs, such as the Mad Dogs. They were the most threatening gang in our area. Their turf was on the other side of College Avenue and, we knew not to go over there alone. Those guys would literally beat you to death. They also used to carry sawed off double barreled shotguns as their trademark. They'd hide the guns under the long trench coats they wore any time of the year. Most of our fights with them ensued when we were either at the bus stop or on our way to or from school. There were times when we would see those guys waiting for us at the bus stop, and if it was more of them than us, we wouldn't go to school. On those days, we'd hang out at someone's house, and they'd smoke marijuana or snort cocaine. They would always ask me to take a hit, but for some reason, I didn't have the desire to.

A lot of times when we played hooky from school, we would go and break into other people's homes. This was done quite frequently. We didn't care whose house we burglarized. There were times when we broke into the homes of some of our closest friends. We would take whatever we could get our hands-on, then we'd sell it. Hot items were easy to get rid of.

One of my closest gang friends was A.J. I guess we were close because our homes were on the same block. A.J. and I were not afraid of anything. We would often just beat up people for the fun of it. You know, sneak up behind them and whip their butts. A.J. got a big kick out of that. A couple of my other partners were Mark and Richard. They were brothers and they loved to rob people. I remember when they robbed a cab driver and an old lady.

John was a member who would do anything. In fact, he would do a lot of things without thinking and would often get caught. You could say I was the thinker of the group. I would normally come up with things for the guys to get into. However, I would never get caught. This was probably because I was never high. Sometimes when we'd do something deviant, those guys would be so high they'd run right into the police. I've seen those guys use just about every type of drug you can name.

At times when we'd cut school we would go to an old house or garage, and they'd do drugs. I'd drink alcohol occasionally and shoot craps as well. Many times, after we'd leave the old garages, we'd end up burning them down. There was a rash of that at one time in Indianapolis.

In spite of us being a gang that stuck together, we'd oftentimes fight each other. I know that I've fought every member of our gang at least four times. Most of the fights against others would usually take place in school. We'd fight white boys in a minute. That was due to them always trying to disrespect us. I don't know about the other guys, but I used to fight white boys a lot, mainly because I was jealous of them. Many of them would come to school dressed nice. Most of them had mothers and fathers in the same house. A lot of times the teachers overtly showed a great deal of favoritism toward them. A white boy could basically get whatever he wanted from a teacher. I couldn't quite understand that. Even black teachers showed white boys more respect than they showed us blacks. I know we were troublemakers and often caused unnecessary problems to people. But, hell, a lot of times we did that because that was the only attention we'd get sometimes. Believe me, sometimes negative attention was better than no attention at all.

It was really difficult growing up as a black male. I never knew a father. The only father that I ever saw was someone else's father. My mother had to work all the time, which I understood and appreciated. The downside to that was it gave me time to be out in the street doing whatever I pleased. During this time of my life, I did not have one positive male role model.

That left the gang as my only source of any family. I loved my sisters, brothers, uncles, and aunts, but they didn't really know how to handle me. Besides, they were too busy with their own lives to even want to handle me anyway.

My oldest brother, Jerry, was a person who I admired a lot; however, he was always in prison. In high school, Jerry was a great athlete. During the end of his senior year, he had gotten a scholarship to play football at Notre Dame. We were so proud of him, especially my mother. Unfortunately, though, about six months before the end of his senior year, my mother sent him downtown to buy my little sister, Pat, a pair of Christmas shoes. In addition to buying the shoes Jerry tried to rob the store. He took a sawed-off shotgun in the store and held them up. As he was leaving, a policeman was entering.

The rest is history.

CHAPTER FOUR
Dumb Fools

Mr. Smith was the shop teacher at our school. He was about five feet five inches tall, well built around fifty years old, with a very deep voice. What made Mr. Smith really unique was that he was our only black male teacher. In fact, I believe he was the only black male teacher I ever saw. Because of that, my friends and I wanted so desperately to get into his class. Most of us were eventually able to enroll in his class and we were very excited, initially.

Mr. Smith was not the black man we thought he'd be. You know, happy that we chose his class and more concerned about us because he understood our lives. Instead, he was the total opposite. He would never smile at us, and always told us that he wasn't going to let us destroy his class.

Once he argued how he had heard about how much trouble we were. "The other teachers told me. Yes, they told me how y'all act stupid and get tossed out of class all the time. Well, I will not have it."

After the first couple of weeks in Mr. Smith's shop class, he stopped talking so much about what problems we caused in the past and started trying to predict how we'd be in the future. And it too, was negative. He held a few of us after class one day and told us that we needed to stop acting like dumb fools.

"Y'all ain't nothing but a bunch of dumb fools. Y'all aren't gonna amount to nothing," he'd say. He reiterated that statement day after day. We really didn't think much of it then, because we had all been told much worse before. It just seemed like Mr. Smith looked forward to us failing in life.

He always talked about the bad things we did and what we needed to stop doing. Never did he try to show us how we should behave. It was this attitude that added to our confusion.

While on the school bus going home one bright, sunny afternoon, we interrupted our usual discussion about what we were going to do for the evening, to discuss Mr.

Smith. Randy spoke of how he thought Mr. Smith was going to be cool at first. John mentioned that he would like to go one-on-one with Mr. Smith in the boxing ring. Mark spoke of how disappointing it was to get criticized by one of our own black people.

"Ain't it enough that we got to put up with white folks calling us fools?"

Big Roland was this overweight kid that was in our class. He wasn't really part of the clique, but he hung out sometimes. Anyway, he felt that maybe Mr. Smith was right.

"Maybe we won't be nothing when we grow up. Hell, look at our neighborhood.

We already did more in life than some of them grown folks," he said disgustingly. "Y'all should know by now it don't matter if a person is white or black, they ain't gonna care about no little black boys from the ghetto," John concluded. "To them we ain't nothing... Nothing but trouble. That's just the way it is, and it always will be.

That's why if we want something in this world, we got to take it, by any means necessary. We ain't nothin' but dumb fools. That's why the teachers don't really try hard to teach us. The grown folks in the neighborhood scared of us, and church folk, hell, they don't even deal with us at all. The only difference between Mr. Smith and the rest of the world is that he don't just think it, he says it. That's why we need each other. That's why we need the gang."

CHAPTER FIVE
No Little Rascals

One day when we were skipping school, we were heading towards one of our hangouts. This particular spot was one of our favorites because it was a big house that was in pretty good shape. However, we were not able to meet there because some people were moving into it. We went down closer to see who was robbing us of our main spot. We didn't know the older people who were carrying boxes into the house; but we recognized the two young boys who were helping them.

"Them two little fools look familiar," John said.

"They should look familiar. Those fools with the Mad Dogs," I said.

"How dare those punks move on this side. They must be out of their minds," said Mark.

I could tell that my guys were highly upset, and they were thinking of some way to retaliate.

"Let's burn down their house," suggested A.J.

I told them that was a stupid idea, and that the best thing to do would be to talk to the brothers and try to get them to flip over and join us. They all agreed that we should try that approach.

Well, a couple of months went by, and we had yet to confront the brothers with our proposition. However, by that time one of the brothers had gotten himself killed. He tried to rob Dave's Variety Store on the corner of 25th and Guilford. I can't believe that fool tried to rob Dave's. He had to be new to the 'hood because everyone in our neighborhood knew not to mess with Dave.

Dave was about fifty years old. He was a Jew. He was basically friendly with everybody in the neighborhood, because he'd give our parents credit. Sometimes he used to give us packs of Now and Laters for staying out of trouble. Dave didn't bother anybody, and even though he trusted most of us, he'd always carry a big 357 Magnum on his side. In fact, he'd have one on his side and another under the cash register. He didn't hesitate to let us see those guns neither. He always said that he didn't want to use them, but if he had to, he wouldn't miss. I could tell that Dave was serious when he said that. The whole neighborhood knew, except, of course, for that new boy. He should've asked somebody before he went in there and tried to rob Dave.

Months later, Dave told me the whole story. He said that the boy walked in, scoped the place out for about five minutes, walked up to the counter, pulled out a gun, and asked him to give up the pistol on his side. The boy then called Big Willie, the butcher, from behind the meat counter and made him take the money out of the cash register, while Dave stood aside. When Big Willie gave him all the money, the boy turned to walk away. It was then that Dave pulled out the second gun from under the counter and blasted that fool in the back. The boy then dropped his gun and the money and fled two blocks to his house. He collapsed and died right on his front steps.

Now that one of the brothers was out of the way we only needed to get the one left to flip. I was told that Richard and John had confronted the guy, but he still refused. I then suggested that we all go and confront him. Then, maybe, he'll see we ain't no punks and do what we ask him.

When we got to his house, all seven of us went up to the door, but before we could knock, the boy pulled up on his bike.

"Yo, man. What's up?" I said.

"Hey, I hope y'all ain't coming around here trying to get me to join that weak Mickey Mouse club y'all call a gang," he said. When he said that, we all got fightin' mad.

"Let's kick that fool's butt, y'all," John said.

Then we all surrounded him. All the other guys started shouting and cursing at the boy.

"Be quiet. He ain't tough," I said. "Look, man," I told him. "All we saying is that since you moved over this way, you should run with us, 'cause we ain't gonna have you livin' on our turf and runnin' with the Dogs."

The guy started mocking us by laughing and once again flat out refused.

"You must think we askin' you to do somethin', you little sissy. We tellin' you," said Mark.

"I tell you what," said John. "You gon' either join us, or you gonna join your stupid brother in hell."

After that, the guy stared at us and walked up to his house. Before he entered the door, he turned and said, "Whatever!" John then threw a brick at the door, and we all ran.

"What you throw that brick for, John?" A.J. asked. "Man, you be doin' some crazy stuff. At least let us know next time."

Throughout the day, we were conjuring up ways to get that dude back for humiliating us and calling us weak. A lot of ideas came by us, such as, burning the house down and doing a drive by. I didn't agree with either, but the gang insisted that we burn the house down. I told them that it wouldn't be a good idea. If we burned the house down the police will easily know it was us. We'll be charged with arson, attempted murder, plus the possibility of having some more arsons and mess pinned on us. Besides, I didn't want to burn the house because the whole family would suffer then. After all, I did see some old people in there when they first moved in. I was the only one opposed to burning the house, but I did finally convince them that it wasn't the thing to do. I persuaded them to just catch the dude out somewhere by himself and beat him until he couldn't talk any more. After we had decided on what course of action we would take to retaliate against this brother, we all left and went our separate ways.

The next day while at school, half the day went by before I realized that I didn't see any of my partners. When I noticed that, I cut my final two classes and went around asking people if they had seen any of the guys. Everyone I asked said no. Then I saw Bobby.

"Bob, you seen any of the boys?"

"Yeah, man, I saw them hanging out in the alley by the gas station on 30th Street this morning. I thought you were with them."

"Oh, my God! I know them idiots ain't gonna go against what I said and burn that house. I know they ain't that stupid."

If they weren't going to burn the house, then why were they on 30th Street by the gas station? We all lived between 23rd and 25th Streets. Plus, they usually told me when they were gonna cut school. Most of the time, I was with them, but this time they didn't tell me anything.

For the remainder of the day while at school, all I could concentrate on was those fools. "Those dummies," I said over and over again. I was beginning to sound like Mr. Smith. When it was finally time to leave school, I ran and jumped on the bus. I didn't say anything during the whole ride home and nobody asked me anything 'cause they knew I had somethin' on my mind. I'm usually the loudest one on the bus.

The house they had talked about burning was on the corner of the 23rd Street bus stop. However, before we could reach that stop, the bus driver was told by a police officer blocking the road that the street had been blocked off. While the bus driver was talking to the policeman, I jumped off the bus and commenced to run full speed towards the house. I didn't have to go far before I noticed the fire trucks, ambulance, and several police cars in front of the house. The house was burning like paper. As I looked at the fire, I felt so afraid. I can't ever remember having that feeling before. I didn't know if someone died or anything. I just couldn't believe that they burned this house down.

What were they thinking? It was at that moment that I realized that there was a big difference between them and me.

As I continued to stand there with several other spectators it appeared as though everything had stood motionless. I finally turned from the crowd and began slowly walking home. I was mesmerized by what had happened. As I thought about it, I felt as though I was walking in slow motion. It was as though I'd been walking for an hour even though I had only made it halfway down the block. All of a sudden, I heard a familiar voice.

"Hey, Jeffrey. Jeffrey, over here."

It was John. He was sitting in the back seat of a police car with his hands behind his back. I ran over to where he was. I then noticed Mark in another police car. Then Richard, A.J. They got all of them! They had them in separate cars. I guess that was so they couldn't communicate and devise some phony story about what happened.

By the time I reached John, I noticed that he had been crying. "Dummies, dummies, dummies," I thought.

"What you crying for, man?" I asked him. With the window of the police car rolled halfway down, I could barely hear him.

"They said they gonna send us to I.Y.C. (Indiana Youth Center)," John said. "They said the police are going to charge us with arson and attempted murder. They said they would think of some more stuff before they got to headquarters." He began to cry again.

I stood there watching John and the rest of my friends in total disbelief. I tell you, for a bunch of guys who were so tough, they didn't look like it today.

A.J. yelled out of the window, "They got us now, don't they, Jeffrey?"

I acknowledged that I heard him, but I didn't answer him. It's too late to ask me for advice. If they'd listened to my advice they wouldn't be in this situation. Suddenly it began to rain. That only added to my solemn mood.

Two weeks had gone by, and I hadn't heard anything about any of the guys. All I knew was that they were still locked up and were likely going to serve several years before they were released.

I didn't know it then, but that would prove to be the last time I saw most of those guys. To this day, I haven't seen Mark. However, I did see Richard briefly five years later, but he was soon arrested again.

This time he went to jail for good. He killed some guy at a pool hall. A.J., my best friend, was released before all the rest, but he was soon admitted to Central State Hospital, an institution for the mentally insane. It was said that he used to sit on his porch naked. It was also speculated that he tried to kill his mother. As for John, he was killed three years later by the police after robbing a liquor store. He was only fifteen.

John's death raised the consciousness of the black community in Indianapolis, because he was so young. It was rumored that he didn't have a gun, and that the officer didn't fire a warning shot.

After those fellas were arrested, however, things were not the same for me at School #61. This was my final year. After this year, I had planned to join my brother, Willie, at Manual High School. There was about one month left for me to go at 61, when I got into a fistfight with my friend, Bobby. He was walking with his new girlfriend this particular day. I ran up to him and thumped him on the top of the head. This was something that we did all the time. I guess since Bobby was with his girl, he wasn't gonna tolerate it.

He swung and hit me very hard in the jaw. Before I knew what happened, we were on the floor fighting. Mr. Smith and a couple more teachers separated us before we seriously injured one another. Mr. Smith grabbed me and one of the other teachers grabbed Bobby. They were escorting us to the principal's office, when I broke loose. Not wanting Bobby to get the best of me, I ran over to hit him, but he ducked. Mr. Smith had positioned himself behind Bobby and I ended up hitting him. I clocked him so hard that I broke his glasses and knocked him into the wall. After I realized that I had hit Mr. Smith, I felt better. I wanted to walk over to him while he was still lying on the floor and say, "You dumb fool."

In spite of being labeled one of the worst kids at School #61, I managed to graduate.

CHAPTER SIX
Cultural Differences

I initially wanted to attend Broad Ripple High School of Performing Arts, because I always wanted to be an actor or comedian. The Performing Arts School would've been a great place to start. However, because my two older brothers attended Manual, my counselor said I had to attend as well. She said that was a new rule.

A week before school was to start, the teachers went on strike. School still started on time, but it was like a joke there those first couple of weeks. Students were roaming around everywhere during all times of the day. My mother said that I didn't really have to go to school if I didn't want to. She felt that because of the strike, I might get hurt or get in some trouble. I insisted on going to school anyway. I enjoyed the freedom of walking around meeting people.

It didn't take long for me to distinguish between high school and middle school. At Manual there were more white students. Also, these white students appeared to be more aggressive. A lot of them strolled around with long hair, beards, and mustaches. They looked much older than they were.

I became a familiar, yet unwelcome, guest of the Dean of Boys, Mr. Lief, real quick. During the first two months of school, I was sent to his office at least five times. Most of the time, it was for fighting, and most of my battles would be with white boys. However, I do remember fighting some black guys too.

My tolerance for whites was very low. I didn't like most of their attitudes. In middle school, when I didn't like someone, I would simply walk up to him and punch him in the jaw as hard as I could.

Most of the time, I'd make sure that a teacher wasn't around. There were times, though, when a teacher's presence didn't interfere with my decision.

I can recall once in middle school when A.J. and I went downtown to shoplift some leather gloves for the sole purpose of fighting white boys. I hit this one boy so hard, that students in the adjacent classrooms heard the noise from the punch. If I had to pinpoint one thing that made me despise white boys back then, I'd have to refer to an incident that occurred in the third grade. I had only been at that school for about a month. We were always being called "niggers," "spooks" and everything else by the white folks there. One day I asked Mrs. Hall, my teacher, for a pass to the restroom. Instead of me going to the little kids' restroom, like I was told, I went to the big kids' restroom. Before I could finish using it, this older white boy came in. First, he asked me what was I doing there. Without giving me a chance to completely answer him, he kicked me in the groin as hard as he could. All I can remember after that was lying on the floor holding myself and crying. I felt oh, so much pain. As I lied there bleeding, I thought to myself that from now on, I'd never let a white boy get the best of me again.

The white boys at Manual didn't just sit around and let you intimidate them. They were quick to fight back. I still would beat them up, regardless of whether they retaliated or not. A lot of times, their retaliation only inspired me to do more damage to them, which to me was just fine. Not only did some of them fight back, they had the audacity to try to pick fights with me. That had never happened in middle school. Most of them undoubtedly knew that I packed a mean butt whippin'. It wasn't long before the students at Manual found that out too.

At the end of my freshman year, I would venture to say that I was sent to Dean Lief's office over thirty times and suspended at least seventeen times. My mother had to come to our school so much that a lot of students thought she was a substitute teacher.

I guess you could say that I was such a big troublemaker at Manual because I was trying to adjust to hanging by myself. My partners were still either in jail or had no intention of coming back to anybody's high school.

In retrospect, I would say the worst white boy that I ever beat up went to Manual.

Believe it or not he asked for it. We were in gym class (one of the only classes that I attended regularly), and the white boys were playing football. I decided to join them. While one boy was throwing the ball to another, I tried to intercept it. At that time, I only wanted to play football. I did not mean any harm. Upon my entering the game and catching the ball, the intended catcher approached me with a mean look on his face.

"What the hell you doin'?" he said. "Nobody asked your black ass to play with us."

He then tried to say something else, but before he could, my fist was introduced to his teeth. I was so upset that I started throwing continuous punches at this boy. Once he fell to the floor, I kicked him in the face a couple of times before the gym teacher tackled me. I was the only one suspended for that.

Most of the time, I started a fight. There was this one fight I was in when my intention was not to actually fight. I only wanted to humiliate the other students. I was in auto shop class, and we were putting lawn mower engines together. Since I had no desire to be a "grease monkey", my interest in that subject was nonexistent. But, since I was there, I had to do something to enjoy myself. I took some oil and placed it on the seats of some of the guys, so when they sat down, they would sit in a tub of oil. It had worked all day, except for this one time.

I placed oil on this big white dude's seat, but before he could sit all the way down, he turned and saw the oil. He then walked over to me with an angry expression. I thought he was going to just wimp out and ask me why I did it like all of the other wimpy white boys. However, to my surprise, he punched me very hard. I mean extremely hard in the mouth. He hit me with so much force that I completely flipped over a table.

Before I could get up off the floor and regain my balance, I heard other students cheering. I finally lifted myself up, but before I could run over and get him, the teacher and some of the students restrained me. The teacher called security and had them escort us separately down the hall to Mr. Lief's office. While I was leaving the room, I heard one white boy laugh, "Yeah! Jeffrey got his butt whipped by a white boy. Good going, dude!"

"He got what he deserved," someone else said.

I was in limbo all that day. When I returned home, I went to the bathroom to look in the mirror. I stared at my swollen lips and bloodstained shirt for a long time. I then started rubbing my lips. They felt numb. I then started feeling to see if my teeth were loose. Sure enough, a couple of them were, and one of them unfortunately fell out right there. I had never been that devastated in my life. I told my mother about it. Out of embarrassment, I stayed in the house for the rest of the day. I felt as though I never wanted to go outside again. This was terrible. How could I ever face my friends or the other kids at school?

When I did return to school, I was getting teased about my missing front tooth.

As a result of that, I got into plenty more fights. My behavior kept getting me suspended from school. During the spring, I was suspended for twenty four days in a row. I don't have to tell you that my grades were awful during my freshman year. My report card read: six F's and a D in gym.

CHAPTER SEVEN
Winds Of Change

My mother was not all that strict on me about my grades. I assume she felt that as long as I went to school, it was all right. Mother didn't receive a lot of schooling herself; however, she was still a very smart woman. After all, she had to be. She brought up twelve kids by herself on a minimum wage salary.

I hated that she had to come to school with me when I got in trouble. That took up a lot of her time. Sometimes, she'd be really tired, but she'd always come to my rescue. No matter how bad I was and how often I was bad, my mother was there for me. Not only did she come to school to rescue me; she'd often have to come to other places as well.

Once I was caught shoplifting from Kroger grocery store. The police officer read me my rights, but before he put me in the police car, he asked me if I had a parent who could come to get me. I phoned my mother, but due to her not having transportation, I was almost sure that she couldn't come the four miles to get me. I was wrong. Somehow, she managed to scrape up enough money to have a cab bring her all that way to get me. I love my mother for those things. Many times, I have said that I would repay her.

On most of the occasions when my mother would come to a store to get me, the police would have already threatened to take me to jail. She'd be so disappointed. I'd never known her to be as upset as she was this particular time. This time she found out more than she could've imagined.

When she arrived at Kroger, the officer brought her to the back of the store where I was being held. He said he asked her back there so that she could see for herself what I was stealing. That day I was caught carrying off at least three cartons of cigarettes and an array of other items. My mother was filled with grief when she saw this.

"What in the world are you doing with these things, son?" she asked. I hesitated before I responded to her.

"I was going to sell them."

What I used to do then was steal a lot of goods from major department and grocery stores and sell them to smaller merchants. Most of the stores that I sold my stolen goods to were in our neighborhood.

I started doing this towards the latter part of my freshman year. I initially stole candy from the grocery stores and sold them to students at Manual. When I sold all of the candy that I had, I would cut class and go back to the store and stock up again. I don't know if I enjoyed making the money or stealing the items the most.

I felt conditioned to steal most of my life, but never to this size. I would do it literally every day after school like therapy. The main items I took were cartons of cigarettes, cologne, jewelry and hair care products. Those were easy to get rid of. There were a couple of variety stores in our neighborhood that solely depended on me to supply those items. I would devise all types of schemes to get away with my shoplifting.

For example, there were times when I'd go into the store and ask the person behind the counter if I could view a particular piece of jewelry. He would give me the jewelry. At that point I would immediately run out of the place. I had confidence that no one could catch me. Sometimes, when I was doubtful, I'd pay some guys that I met at school to stand outside the doors and distract the person who was chasing me. They'd usually be some big black guys that would open a hole for me to run through just like a football player. When the person from the store would try to follow me, they'd close the gap and keep them from coming through. Most of the time the man pursuing me would be a white man. When he'd notice several big black guys standing outside, he would often curtail his pursuit and return hurriedly to his establishment.

My level of shoplifting escalated when I was twelve years old. I was now more relentless. Not only was I relentless with it, but with fighting as well. I guess that in regard to the latter, I was more cautious now. I now knew that I could be beaten, and I was going to do all that I could not to allow that to happen. One thing that I would do to prevent myself from losing a fight would be to spray mace in my opponent's face before I started to drill him with my fists. By doing this, I was guaranteed to win. But there was one thing I had to be aware of when using this method. Retaliation.

I never knew spraying mace in peoples' eyes could make them so angry. There were times when I was shot at, and a couple of times when I was jumped on and beaten down because of this. Once when I was jumped on, I was left with a black eye, a huge knot on my head, and one hundred fifty stitches in my back. My mother would often tell me that if I kept doing the things that I was doing, I wouldn't live to see my eighteenth birthday. What she said had an effect on me. I stopped fighting as much, but I just couldn't stop shoplifting.

Most of the shoplifting that I did during this time in my life, I did alone. That was until I met my new friends Jake and Tuffy. Neither of them knew anything about shoplifting. Jake was a so-called "pretty boy" whose only purpose in life was to get as many girls as he could. Tuffy was a mama's boy. I don't really remember how we met, but I know it didn't take long for us to become best friends. When we first met, we would hang out downtown after school, play video games and mess with girls. It wasn't long before I introduced them to my world of shoplifting.

I knew that it wouldn't be easy getting these guys to accept my slick way of stealing, so I had to break them in gently. I started them out by getting them to steal something I knew they were interested in. Since they were both video game junkies, I started them out by showing them how to steal quarters to play video games.

This was the scheme. We'd take a five-dollar bill, write on it, and put it in the change machine. Then, five dollars in quarters would fall from the machine. We'd take four dollars' worth of quarters, give them to a friend to hide in his pocket, and then tell the operator of the machine that we put a five dollar bill in it but were only given a dollar's worth of quarters. The operator would open the machine and find that a

five-dollar bill would be on the top. If he'd ask about the five-dollar bill, I'd tell him that it was written on, and continue to describe the writing. I had them going to various change machines throughout the downtown area to work this game.

Jake and Tuffy were mesmerized by my style. They'd often want to go with me when I shoplifted. After showing those guys how to steal quarters, I then introduced them to taking clothing. Since Jake was a ladies' man, he was more interested in stealing clothing than Tuffy. Jake always needed to dress nice for the ladies. Tuffy was more impressed with making quick money. His obsession with making money led him to do things on his own, like selling marijuana. For some reason I was never interested in selling marijuana or any other drugs. I often told Tuffy to be careful and to make sure he knew his clientele before making a sell or a buy.

Towards the end of my sophomore year at Manual, I was becoming disinterested in the shoplifting game. I don't know what was happening, but I was losing my zeal to steal. Believe it or not I was even considering joining Bobby's church. The thought was short-lived, due to the fact that once I did decide to go to church, I overheard an official of the church, who happened to live in my neighborhood, tell Bobby, "Why did you bring that bad boy to this church?"

After hearing that, I felt as though I was not welcome there, and thus, never went with him again.

Jake used to go to church every Sunday with his aunt. I was never interested in going to church with them because they'd spend all day there.

I had never been forced to go to church in my life, nor had I ever been a member of any church. The thought of my attending church seemed ridiculous, so, I put it behind me and continued to do what I did best: shoplift and fight.

I must have taken things from every store downtown but was never arrested. Lately, though, I was beginning to get a little rusty. One time Tuffy and I stole some jewelry out of this major department store. As we were leaving the store, the police began to chase us. We both ran out of the store and fled down the street. Two police cars then joined in the chase. We ran two blocks crossing traffic trying to dodge them.

I simply wanted to outrun those cops, but Tuffy persuaded me to hide behind a trash dumpster in an alley. As we hid behind it, the police rode right pass us. We then continued to flee the officers by running in the opposite direction. We soon found ourselves blocked in by a huge barbed wire fence. We knew we had to climb it, because we were certain that the police would come back this way.

On the other side of the fence was the bus stop. If we climbed over, we'd be home free. Tuffy proceeded to climb first. He took off his jacket and laid it across the top of the fence to keep from getting cut. I then removed my sweater and did the same. I was almost over the fence, when all of a sudden, OUCH! I felt a wire enter my stomach. It was an awful pain. I then fell to the other side. Although I was hurting pretty badly, I knew that I had to continue to run in order to escape that area before the authorities arrived.

We then noticed a bus coming. Not caring where it was headed, we were going to get on it. Once on the bus, I knew we were free. It was then that I began to pay attention to the wound in my stomach. It wasn't bleeding much, but it appeared to be very deep. I could see the white meat. I was certain that I would need stitches.

When I made it home, I was in so much pain that I could hardly stand up. I walked in the house holding my stomach and bleeding. My family thought I had been shot. I explained to them that I was out fooling around and tried to jump a fence when I was caught by a barbed wire. No one questioned my story. They were mainly concerned with getting me to a hospital.

Jerry drove me to the hospital. When we arrived, I was at once taken to a room. The doctor looked at my injury and informed us that I'd definitely need stitches. At that time, tears began to flow from by eyes. I was not crying because of my pain. I was crying because I was simply tired of coming to the hospital, tired of getting in trouble, tired of having to run from people and tired of doing wrong.

I lied there on my back as the doctor began to stitch me up. All I could imagine was coming in this hospital and having to be carried out through the back door. I knew that it would be a matter of time before my actions would cause me to enter this building just to leave in a wooden box. The thing that I thought about most was what my mother said.

"Boy, you ain't gonna live to see your eighteenth birthday. Boy, you ain't gonna live to see your eighteenth birthday..."

I knew I needed to change. I knew I wanted to change, but I didn't know how. All I've ever known was how to do wrong and how to hurt people. No one had ever really presented me with a good reason to make a change. Of course, while in school, certain people would come to visit and talk to us about doing the right things and making the right choices in life. But, hell, after that we wouldn't see them again. At this point I really do have the desire to change. It is only now, when I lay in a hospital bed, that I seriously consider my future. I was willing to take the steps necessary to change my life.

The next couple of weeks proved, however, that transforming my life wouldn't be easy. I had gotten in two more fights and continued to supply our neighborhood stores with stolen goods. In spite of my continuing down my path of mischief, I often pondered about what it would be like to be on the right side of the law. That idea was still just a thought in my mind. It was a thought that was easy to dream about, but very difficult to truly conceptualize. One reason for that was because there wasn't anyone in my life to pattern myself after. Oh, I almost forgot. There was Mr. Gibson. He was literally almost a hundred years old. He used to be a reporter for the Indianapolis Recorder. He wrote articles every now and then on an old typewriter he kept in his dining room. He was about 6'3", very dark, with short white hair. He walked slowly and bent over.

I met him while I was washing my uncle's car in front of our house one day. He lived across the street. He often asked me to go to the store for him. We became good friends. He would always give me money for Christmas and made sure that I had a good pair of shoes. He said that shoes said a lot about a person.

Mr. Gibson never tired of giving me advice, whether I wanted it or not. He'd tell me things like, "Boy, you better stop going out there stealing and fighting. You keep that up, you gon' go to hell just as sure as you standing there."

I don't know how he knew what I was doing. It was almost like he was reading my mind. Our friendship only lasted three years because of his death.

I was saddened by Mr. Gibson's death. He was the closest thing I had to an advisor. In spite of his good advice, I hadn't paid much attention to it until now, now that I do seek to become a better person.

As time went on, and I continued doing the things that I knew I shouldn't, I began to challenge my will to do right. For some reason, I wasn't getting the same thrill in stealing, and fighting wasn't exciting anymore. Actually, I found myself for the first time beginning to back down from a fight and to avoiding confrontations altogether. My desire to change my ways came about in short spans, because once I got around Jake and Tuffy, I would begin to shoplift again.

The reason for doing it this time was not based on the greed of acquiring a certain item, but to impress Jake and Tuffy. They admired me for stealing and often tried to emulate my style. Jake would observe me shoplift, then he'd do it, but most of the time I tried to discourage him from doing it because he was not as polished. Tuffy, on the other hand, was street smart and began to remind me of myself with his smooth way of taking what didn't belong to him. In fact, Tuffy began to get carried away with making fast money so much so, that he had gotten to the point where not only was he stealing, but selling more marijuana and even this new drug, crack. I thought about joining him, but I knew that if I had, I would get hooked and eventually allow it to destroy me. Since I didn't want to sell drugs, my friendship with Tuffy began to weaken. Jake and Tuffy's friendship died down as well because Jake didn't have the guts to sell drugs, although, he did get starry-eyed when he saw the wad of money that Tuffy began to flash around.

SECTION TWO
"Discovering God"

CHAPTER EIGHT
Looking For Strength

I couldn't believe it. This was the second semester of my third year of high school, and I hadn't been sent to the dean's office at all this year. It was a big difference from my freshman year. My grades even began to improve. One day while I was sitting in class the teacher called me up to her desk.

"Jeffrey, you have to go to the principal's office," she said. "The principal's office? What for? I didn't do anything." "I don't know. Just go," she said.

As I was walking to the principal's office, I tried to figure out why he wanted to see me. I had never been to the principal's office. Whenever a student got into trouble, he'd go to see the dean, not the principal.

I know what it is. Somebody set me up. No, he wants to see me for something I did a long time ago, and they forgot to punish me.

I didn't know what it was. I was going crazy trying to figure out what I had done. When I arrived at the office, the principal's secretary directed me to his door. I nervously opened it. As I entered, I saw this white-haired man reading through a stack of papers that were stacked on his desk. He slowly raised his head.

"You must be Jeffrey Thomas," he said.

"Yes, sir, I am." The principal then began to shuffle several sheets of computer paper.

"Mr. Thomas," he said, "I see here that you've really cleaned up your act. A couple of years ago, you were suspended seventeen times. This year, however, you've never been suspended, nor have you been to the office for any disciplinary problem. Not only that, but your grades. As a freshman, you had six F's and one D. This year you have all C's. I'd like to know what caused this transition. It was predicted that you would be one of the several students that we would have to drop out."

"Well, sir. I just want to do better. I don't find much pleasure in the things I used to do."

He then asked me if I had joined a church or had any religious influences. "Not really," I told him. "However, I do have a friend who attends church with his aunt every Sunday. I've gone with them a couple of times."

The principal continued to congratulate me on my new conduct and concluded by mentioning that he saw potential in me. He told me that I should consider going to church more.

"Thank you, sir. Thank you, a lot." I left his office with a big smile on my face.

I was ecstatic about meeting with the principal. All that day I was happy. I felt like I had won the lottery. Never had anyone complimented me for doing well. It was an exceptionally welcomed feeling. This was the catalyst for my spiritual transition.

Three weeks had passed, and on each of those past Sundays I went to church with Jake and his family. It had gotten to the point where I began to look forward to churching. Nonetheless, I often felt out of place while in service. I'd look around and notice all of the well-dressed people and those pretty girls. Sometimes I wondered what I was doing there. If these people knew what type of person I was, they'd kick me clean out of this place. After all, this was not just any place of worship I was attending. This was St. John Missionary

Baptist Church on the corner of 17th and Martindale. I had heard a lot about this place. It was the most popular church in the city among black folks.

Every Sunday at eleven o'clock, they'd come on the radio and have service. They were also on the radio on Saturdays. Each Saturday at noon Operation Bread Basket was held there. This would be when the political figures, both black and white, would come together and discuss certain community programs or other issues.

I became weary of that big church, although I continued attending, because I believed that they'd never accept me. I thought about joining another church, but I kind of enjoyed going to St. John with Jake and his aunt. She'd always have a big dinner ready for us afterwards. Jake's aunt's name was Helen. She treated me like family, even when she got wind of how bad I used to be. She always showed me affection. She also began to witness to me more. One thing about her was she didn't hide behind anything. She'd tell it like it was.

"Boy, you need to go on and join church. You also need to start testifying sometimes. Ain't nothing in the street for you," she'd say in a motherly voice. I was gradually getting used to this church thing. Aunt Helen was really beginning to have an effect on my being comfortable there. I still wasn't ready to stand up and talk in front of all those people.

One Sunday as Jake and I sat in the balcony and listened to the pastor, Dr. Andrew J. Brown, preach, I noticed myself really starting to pay attention. I would hear him every Sunday, but this time I was not just hearing, I was listening.

"Matthew 6:24 states: "No man can serve two masters, for either he will hate the one, and love the other; or else he will hold to the one and despise the other. Ye cannot serve God and man." But we must choose. Who will you choose?" preached Dr. Brown.

"Who will you choose?" was the thought that repeatedly entered my mind all week. This was a strange period in my life, because not only was I thinking about church more, I was dreaming about it. I can recall one dream that I had that was really deep. I envisioned that I had died and gone to hell. It was horrible. I saw my life pass before me. I noticed all of the things that I was doing wrong. I began to miss my family, my dear loving mother, my brothers and sisters. This dream was very clear to me. I'd begun to understand how simple it was to choose Jesus. "Who will you choose?"

I awoke that morning in a cold sweat. What was happening? I couldn't clearly understand.

Later that day when I went to school, Tuffy approached me and asked me to go to the grocery store with him. I knew what that meant. Every time we went to the grocery store, it would be to steal candy or something that we could sell. I hardly ever turned down the opportunity to go with him, and I didn't turn it down this time either. We entered the grocery store as we normally did-- me first, and five minutes later he'd come in. Usually, by the time he'd come in I would be loaded down with stolen goods and heading out the door.

Today, however, that was not the case. I was just walking around the store contemplating what move I should make next. I felt strange, stranger than ever. Then came Tuffy. He came in early this time. He was walking towards me while I stood in the candy aisle.

"What's up?" he asked. "You got somethin' yet?" "No," I told him.

"Damn, Jeffrey. You losin' your touch ain't you? This whole aisle would've been emptied by now." He then turned and went away.

Tuffy was very bold, sometimes too bold. For instance, as he turned from me, he picked up a big bag of candy bars and stuck them in his pants. It was as if he didn't care who saw him. After he made his move, I knew it was my turn. It was time for me to put up or shut up. I reached for the candy bars. When I gripped them, I held on to them before I picked them up. This day I was feeling different. I knew I would be doing something wrong if I stole this candy. I never used to think about or care about if I was doing wrong in the past.

I tried to pick up the candy, but it was as if I was picking up a ton of bricks. I couldn't do it. All of a sudden "Who will you choose?" flashed across my mind. Who will you choose? Do you want this candy, or do you want Jesus? Before I could even clear that thought, I let go of the candy and walked out of the store emptyhanded.

I was ecstatic when I reached the parking lot. I actually felt good for not stealing. "Thank you, Jesus," I said. For the first time in my life, I said "Thank you, Jesus." Two weeks had gone by, and I hadn't stolen anything at all. I also hadn't seen

Tuffy since that day. I later found out that the reason for my not seeing him was because he had gotten arrested and sent to juvenile hall. That's right, he had been caught for stealing that candy.

He told me the whole story the next time I saw him. He said that as he was leaving the store, a police officer followed him. The officer flashed his badge and grabbed him by the collar of his shirt. Somehow, he managed to get away and ran two blocks before he was apprehended. In an attempt to escape, he cut through someone's backyard. There he pulled the stolen items out of his pants and dropped them on the ground. When the police caught up to him, they were going to let him go, because he didn't have the evidence on him. However, just before they released him, a little white boy came from behind the house where Tuffy dropped the candy. This little boy had the candy in his hand.

"Excuse me," he said as he approached Tuffy and the officers. "Mister, you dropped this in our yard."

Tuffy spent two weeks in juvenile because his mother refused to come get him. He said that if I'd stolen some candy, I would've been caught too because the officer said that I was also being watched. Once again, I say, "Thank you, Jesus." Not only would accepting the word of God keep you from going to hell, but it could also keep you from going to jail!

CHAPTER NINE
The Testimony

"And they overcame him by the blood of the Lamb and by the word of their testimony" -Rev. 12:11 NIV

It was the summer before my senior year of high school. Several months had gone by since Tuffy's unfortunate experience. During this time, I was sort of a loner. I was hanging by myself, except on Sundays, when I'd go to church with Jake. I hadn't missed a Sunday all during this time. I started going to church on Monday evenings too. The church had initiated a youth program that Jake and I became members of. This auxiliary really helped me to focus more on Jesus Christ and His will for my life. A young preacher named Steve Mitchell administered it.

Rev. Mitchell wasn't much older than me, but he could really preach. I especially liked Rev. Mitchell because he'd add humor to his style of teaching. One of the questions Rev. Mitchell would ask us was "How many of y'all know beyond a shadow of a doubt that if you died today, you would go to heaven?"

I would never raise my hand at this question. There were still some areas in my life that needed cleaning up. I hadn't stolen anything for three or four months. I hadn't been in a fight in about nine months. That was a great accomplishment for me, but there were still some things I needed to work on. Having this newfound understanding of God was very different for me and was going to take some time to adjust. I'm not where I want to be yet, but I'm gonna giving it all I got. I must give my all, because I didn't want to fight anymore. I was satiated with having to watch my back everywhere I went.

Going to church seemed to be the way out for me.

This may be just what I need. After all, I wasn't a terribly bad person. I just never took advantage of any other alternatives. Now I am. I can go to church, accept Jesus into my life, and live happily ever after. At least, that's what I was told.

I found myself spending more and more time around St. John. Rev. Brown even knew my name, and often he'd ask me to do things for him around the church. My mother was shocked at how often I went.

"You must have a girlfriend around there," she said. It wasn't that, however, I didn't bother to tell her my reasons. I wanted her to notice a change for herself.

Oh, yes! I'm gonna change. I know there is something good inside of me, and I will seek to bring it out. I felt this way because I had visions-- dreams about me speaking in church in front of the whole congregation. Although I dreamed it, it was very unlikely to come true any time soon. For one thing, besides my being flat out nervous when it came to speaking in public, I was embarrassed because I had a missing front tooth.

But, one thing's for sure. My unproductive activities in the neighborhood began to decrease. I'd normally hang out with Bobby and Tuffy while they stood on the corner of 23rd Street and drank MD 20/20 and sold nickel and dime bags of marijuana. Tuffy was getting pretty big in the dope game, so he wasn't hanging on the corner as much, plus he began making runs for the big boys.

Once while walking past them on the corner, they stopped me.

"Jeffrey, what's up with you, man? Why you don't be chillin' no more?" asked Bobby.

"I just been busy, man. I ain't had no time."

"No, fool, I know what it is. You been down at that big church with Jake tryin' to get some girls, haven't you? I want to go next time," he said.

I told Bobby that I'd like for him to come to church with us. Something that I didn't quite understand was that he used to be a good guy when he was younger. He was a Jehovah's Witness and attended the Kingdom Hall regularly. You could hardly catch him without his Bible. Now look at him on the corner selling drugs.

I thought about this a lot. I wondered if the same thing would happen to me.

Whatever turned him around could probably turn me around. What made me better than him? Just the thought of selling drugs frightened me. At our next youth meeting at church, I explained Bobby's situation to Rev. Mitchell.

"Rev. Mitchell, what makes people turn away like that? I thought God would keep that from happening to you." I figured Rev. Mitchell would have a good response to this. It was like he was blessed to answer this type of question.

He began to explain to me about how Jesus used a parable that said something about how the Word of God is sometimes like a seed. He referred me to Luke 8:58:

"A Sower went out to sow his seed; and as he sowed, some fell by the wayside; and it was trodden down, and the fowls of the air devoured it. And some fell upon a rock: and as soon as it was sprung up, it withered away, because it lacked moisture. And some fell among thorns and the thorns sprang up with it and choked it. And others fell on good ground and sprang up and bare fruit a hundredfold."

"How can my seed be planted on good ground?" I asked.

Rev. Mitchell explained how I needed to pray more, read my Bible, and something about proclaiming the gospel of Jesus Christ.

"Proclaiming the gospel? Is that like speaking in front of people?" I asked. "Yes. It's like speaking about Christ wherever you go."

"If that's what it takes," I said.

The next week during Wednesday night prayer service, Rev. Brown asked if anybody had any testimonies.

"Does anybody want to stand up and thank the Lord today?" he asked.

Three old ladies stood up and spoke about how the Lord did this and did that for them. After they spoke, no one else stood up. The place was silent, as Rev. Brown looked around to see if there was anyone else with a testimony.

"Is there anyone?" Before he could finish, I was on my feet. "Yes, Jeffrey?

Go ahead," he said with a smile.

What have I done? I didn't mean to stand up. It's too late now. Now, I just had to say something.

"Well I, I'd just like to thank God for allowing me to get out of the gang before it was too late. And, I thank him for letting me come to this church. And . . . Thank y'all."

As I sat down, I felt relieved. I looked to my left and there was Rev. Mitchell, smiling with a thumbs-up sign. After service I was surprised to hear that many people were impressed with what I said. Older people approached me to say that they were going to pray for me.

"Hang in there, young man," they said. "Keep up the good work."

After that, whenever the opportunity arose, I'd give a testimony. The least I could do was thank God for waking me up. I noticed that with each testimony I'd give, the more the church folks embraced me. One day after Sunday service, Rev. Brown called me into his office. He said that next Sunday would be Youth Sunday. He asked me if I would stand in the pulpit and give my personal testimony in front of the whole church. I told him that I would. However, when I got home, I regretted it.

"The whole church?" Jake asked after I told him what was asked of me. "Boy, you must be crazy. Do you know how many people will be at church on Sunday? At least two thousand."

I became nervous about this whole thing, but I had already made the commitment.

I invited my mother and the rest of my family to come to church with me that day. I wanted my mother to come especially because I did not want her to have any doubts about my sincerity to the Lord.

The time had come. As I sat in the pulpit waiting for my turn, the youth choir sang "What a Friend We Have in Jesus." The congregation was full. It didn't look like there was one empty seat in that big two-story church. I sat there scanning the audience. There was Jake, his aunt and Rev. Mitchell. Everyone was there. My mother sat in the second row behind the mourners' bench.

The choir finally stopped singing and Rev. Brown approached the podium. My name was next on the itinerary. Rev. Brown made a couple of comments about how well the choir sang before he called me up.

"Now we have a young man who recently joined this church," said Rev. Brown. It was my turn. I felt so nervous. "Now to give his personal testimony, we have Jeffrey Thomas."

I got up to the podium, cleared my throat and began to speak.

"I, first, thank God, and I thank Rev. Brown. All I want to say is that I'm thankful to be standing here today instead of lying in a casket somewhere. My mother told me a long time ago that if I kept doing wrong, that's where I'd be. Well, I stand here today in the presence of God and my mother and say, Momma, I know I've caused you a great deal of pain. I know there were times when you came to school for me when you didn't feel like it. I know there were times when you stayed up all night wondering if I was gonna make it home. Well, Momma, I stand here to tell you, you ain't gotta worry about that no more. Momma, I don't need to cause trouble in school no more to get attention, because I now have a friend that'll always give me attention. Momma, I don't need to steal no more to get what I want, because I got a friend now who gives me what I want and more. Momma, for all the pain that I've caused you, I'm sorry. Thanks to my new friend, Jesus Christ, you ain't got to worry about that no more."

As I began to turn and go to my seat, the whole congregation stood up. They clapped and smiled. My mother started to cry; so, did my brother, June. I felt good knowing that something I said made them react this way. What I had said was true. I believed that I now had a new friend. I was so engulfed with my speech about Jesus that it was all I thought about. I forgot about my missing front tooth until I sat down. But even at that, I wasn't embarrassed.

CHAPTER TEN
The Fight

I had begun to volunteer my services around the church often. Rev. Mitchell and some of the other employees at St. John would invite me to lunch and other special events. My inner spirit began to grow each day, and I began to feel a love for God. I believed that all of my mischievous acts were behind me. That was, until this particular day.

Jake, Tuffy, and I were in an arcade playing a video game while we waited for the bus. I was playing Ms. Pac Man and my game had just ended. Since Jake and Tuffy were still into their games, I decided to go outside to see if the bus was coming.

I casually walked out onto the curb. As I did, I could hear the music blasting from the speakers on the roof of the neighborhood variety store.

"Nope, I don't see no bus."

Reentering the arcade, I noticed a couple of guys follow me in. Before I could turn around, BAM! Instantly, I was pushed from behind. This was a very hard push. It was so forceful that I hit the counter and fell onto the floor. I lay there for a minute to catch my breath. I got up and turned and saw the two guys. I did not recognize them.

"What's goin' on? What you pushed me for?"

"You know why, you punk," one guy said. "You robbed me last week when I came up here." I knew this was a clear mistake. This guy thought I was someone else.

"Hey, I ain't done nothin', man. I don't even live around here."

"You a damn lie. Bring yo' butt outside so I can finish what I started."

I didn't have any intentions on fighting, and I wanted to straighten this thing out.

I walked over to Jake.

"Hey, Jake, explain to this brother that I don't live around here," I said.

Jake approached the bully and before he could get anything out of his mouth to defend me, POW! The dude hit him in the mouth knocking him to the floor.

"He hit Jake," Tuffy said. I then felt that I had no other option than to protect myself.

I followed this guy towards the door, but before I reached it, I heard Tuffy scream from behind me.

"Don't go out there, Jeffrey! He has a gun!" I quickly turned around and helped Jake off the floor. "He ain't got no gun," someone said. At this point all of us were angry.

"Let's go get 'em," Jake said. I rushed behind Jake outside. I couldn't dare let him fight these thugs alone. After all, Jake was about six feet, two inches and weighed about one hundred fifty pounds.

Once we got outside, the guys were standing there waiting. Jake reached into the trash can right outside the door and took a bottle out of it. His intentions were to break the bottle and use the remains as a weapon. When he tried to break the bottle on the sidewalk, the whole thing shattered leaving only the cap of it in his hand. Frustrated about this, he threw the cap at one of the guys causing them both to only laugh.

One guy rushed me and shoved me into the wall of the arcade. Well, that's it.

I have no other choice. I grabbed the guy by his waist and threw him on the ground. I then hit him in the face with my fist. He got up and tried to rush me again. This time I grabbed his hair and kneed him in the face. I did this about four more times before the guy lost consciousness.

I looked to my right and saw Jake getting beat down by the other guy. I didn't see Tuffy anywhere, so I decided to go and help Jake. Before I could reach him, I felt an object strike me in the eye. I fell to the ground. By the time I regained my balance, the fight was over, and the guys were gone.

"Are they gone yet?" asked Tuffy, as he stuck his head out from around the building.

Later that day I felt bad about what happened. Even though I didn't start it this time, I was upset about it. How could I have fought those guys? I was supposed to be a new person. I recalled reading in II Corinthians 5:17, "Therefore, if anyone is in Christ, he is a new creation; the old has gone, the new has come." (NIV)

How could I be a new creation if I was still engaging in my old ways? I was distraught about this situation. Therefore, I told my friend and mentor Rev. Mitchell about it. Rev. Mitchell once again brought clarity to my situation and made it so that I didn't feel so bad.

In spite of Rev. Mitchell's spiritual comforting, I still apologized to the guy I fought two weeks later when I saw him again. When I did, he didn't know what I was talking about. That could've been because he was stoned. As I spoke to him that day, I clearly saw the damage that I had done to him during the fight. I did more than I thought. He was really bruised up.

CHAPTER ELEVEN
Faith

Summer was finally coming to an end. All summer long I had been praying to the Lord to make it possible for me to transfer to Broad Ripple High School. Most people called it Ripple for short.

Ripple was totally different from Manual because it was predominately black. It also had a reputation for being the high school where fashion was just as important as education. My reasons for wanting to transfer had nothing to do with the black population or the fashion. I wanted to go because they had the only Performing Arts school in the city, and as I said I always wanted to be an actor or comedian. Because I was seeking to be the best Christian that I could possibly be, a new school would be best. There were too many bad memories at Manual. Also, I had too many old buddies who wouldn't understand my new attitude, and thus would try to convince me to do wrong.

I prayed to God so much asking Him to bless me to go to Broad Ripple, that I know He must have been tired of me. I had a lot of faith that God would make this happen. After all, it was because of my true desire to get to know Him that I sought this change.

One day as I lay in the bed, I heard the Lord answer my prayer.

"You will go to the Broad Ripple School of Performing Arts." This was the first time that I'd ever heard the Lord speak to me so clearly. After that, I had no doubt in my mind that I'd be in Ripple by the fall. I had not yet been accepted, but I knew it would happen, because God told me.

I knew that in order to attend Broad Ripple you had to go through an audition. I called the school and a man by the name of Mr. Patrick answered. He was the director of the Performing Arts School. He scheduled an interview date for me. Mr. Patrick knew who I was because I tried to enter this school twice before, but to no avail.

The audition was scheduled for next Saturday. School would be starting in less than a month. I would be auditioning for the Drama department. It was mandatory for me to do two skits one serious and one comedy.

On the day of the audition, I was pretty confident. I had been rehearsing every day with my little sister, Pat. The audition was held in Ripple's auditorium. When I entered, the place was very gloomy. You could barely see the stage.

"Welcome, Mr. Thomas," a voice said from one of the aisles.

"Hey, you scared me," I said, as I noticed Mr. Patrick and some lady sitting with note pads in their hands.

"I'm glad you're on time. You're the only one auditioning today so go get yourself prepared, and let us know when you're ready," he said.

I came from backstage several minutes later.

"I'm ready, sir." It's meant for me to be on stage, I thought. I performed, then, finally, the whole thing was over. "Great job, Mr. Thomas. Call us early Monday."

"Yes, sir." I happily packed my gear and headed out of the door. I told my family that I did well. I was so confident with my performance that I told Jake, Tuffy, and everyone else that I was accepted to the School of Performing Arts, even before it was announced. I wasn't worried.

After all, the Lord said I would be enrolled in this school. Plus, my audition went well. There was no way I could've been turned down.

Today was the big day. It was five minutes after nine, Monday morning. Mr. Patrick arrives at his office at nine o'clock. I couldn't wait to hear him say that I was admitted. I didn't sleep well at all last night anticipating this moment.

The phone was ringing. It must have rung for five minutes before there was an answer.

"Hello?" came the voice from the other end. It sounded like Mr. Patrick. "Hi. I'm Jeffrey Thomas."

"Yes, Mr. Thomas. I was expecting your call," said Mr. Patrick. "Young man, we both enjoyed your audition. You do have talent, and we're glad that you have an interest in the Broad Ripple School of Performing Arts. However," Before he could go any further, I interrupted him.

"Mr. Patrick, I have been interested in this school for three years. This would be my dream if I was accepted there."

"Yes, Jeffrey, I understand. However, I regret to inform you that because you are a senior, it would be difficult for you to catch up with the other kids. Therefore, we can't accept you into this school's Drama department. We wish"

"But, Mr. Patrick, I'll work extra hard. I'd do anything."

"I'm sorry Jeffrey. Have a nice day," he said before he hung up the phone. How could this happen? How could this happen after I had that great audition? Besides, I had the dream. The Lord told me that I'd be accepted. What's going wrong?

All day I pondered on what Mr. Patrick said. Since I'm a senior, it'd be difficult for me to catch up. That's nonsense. If that were the case, they wouldn't have let me audition in the first place. What am I going to tell everyone? I already told them that I got in.

I stayed in seclusion all day. I just sat in my bedroom, which I shared with three other family members. I hoped no one would come in.

"How could this happen, Lord?" I asked. I started praying. I must have prayed a hundred times that day. I wasn't mad at God, and I told him that. However, I was disappointed. I told the Lord that I loved Him and that I still wanted to know Him better, but I didn't understand Him telling me I'd be accepted to Broad Ripple when I wasn't.

Another day passed and I was again secluded in my room. I just didn't want to go back to Manual, but since it looked like I'd have to, I got prepared for it. I started going through some of my old notebooks that I had stored away in the closet. I salvaged through my math books, English books, art books, and science books. Each of those classes was mandatory, except for art.

I took art classes because I loved to draw. Ever since third grade I'd draw various images. My gift to draw was actually discovered in sixth grade when I won an art exhibition. That was neat. As a result of my winning, I was able to take a whole day out of school to go to the Indiana Art Museum. I still remember that. It was fun. At one time, I thought about being an artist, but that thought didn't last long. Someone once told me that an artist didn't become successful until after they died.

While I was reminiscing about my art experiences, I stumbled across a brochure about Ripple's School of Performing Arts. I noticed on the front cover pictures of people acting, dancing, singing, and what else?

Drawing! I opened the brochure to the page that featured drawing. At the top of the page it stated, "We also have a Visual Arts department." Hey, maybe I could get into this. After all I do remember hearing Mr. Patrick saying that they couldn't have me in the Drama department.

I called Mr. Patrick the next day. He listened to what I had to say about the Visual Arts department. He asked me to bring in some of my work.

"Do you have at least seven pieces of artwork to bring in?" he asked.

"Yes, sir! Yes, sir!" With as much drawing as I did, I easily had seven pieces.

I took my drawings to his office the next day. He was so impressed that he didn't believe that I drew the pictures. As a result, he said that he'd have to give me a test before he could make a decision. He then escorted me to an empty room, gave me two large blank sheets of paper and told me what he wanted me to draw. He said that I had to use the different colored pieces of chalk he provided. He gave me one hour.

In thirty minutes, I was finished drawing what he asked. I used various colors and was satisfied with the art.

"Done already?" Mr. Patrick asked me as I entered his office. I gave him my work and waited on his response. "Well, Mr. Thomas today is your lucky day. We do have room for you in our Visual Arts class, and your talent is definitely good enough for me to approve you. Congratulations."

I rushed home and told my family and hurried to my room to thank God. God was right. I would be accepted to the School of Performing Arts. I didn't see it happening at first, but He did. Thank you, Jesus, was all I could say. I had been told to trust in the Lord and He would not fail me. This was a great example of that.

A Change In High Schools

As soon as I entered the doors of this new facility, I knew my life would be different. My confidence level was very high at this time. I was involved in a new school. All of the problems I had at Manual were left behind. No more fighting, no more stealing, no more failing classes, and no more Dean's office. This was it for me.

My first month was exciting. I made several new friends and was reunited with some old ones from middle school. Jake and Tuffy had also transferred to this school. But, Tuffy hardly ever came. He was still preoccupied with making a quick dollar. He was so into making money that he would flaunt wads of it around to try to impress our new friends. On the other hand, all Jake was consumed with was trying to see how many girls he could win over. I had dated a few girls here and there in the past, but being mischievous took precedence over them. Now, a girl would be just right for me a Christian girl, that is.

It wasn't long before I met that special someone. Her name was Alicia. We spent every evening after school together. She was the best thing, besides Jesus, that could have happened to me. Alicia came from a strict family; therefore, the time we spent together was usually in school. I was really comfortable with her, and I told her everything there was to know about me; including how I used to run with thugs and how I would steal merchandise to make a profit.

I can remember her telling me that it was difficult for her to believe that I was once that way because I seemed to be so friendly. I had been hearing that a lot lately. People would often tell me how nice I was. After my first six weeks of school, when the report cards came out, not only did Alicia think I was nice, but smart too. This was even hard for me to believe. I made the honor roll. Never, ever, in my life had I made the honor roll until now. I had been praying that my grades improved. By concentrating on improving my life spiritually, my grades got better too. I guess they go hand in hand.

As all of these good things happened to me, my faith in Jesus Christ increased. In fact, it grew so much that I began to tell others about what the Lord was doing for me.

"You are the light of the world. A city that is set on a hill cannot be hidden. Nor do they light a lamp and put it under a basket, but on a lamp stand . . . Let your light shine before men." Matthew 5:14-16 (NIV)

A lot of times when I praised God's name in school, I was met with opposition.

That was okay, though, because I recall reading in the Bible where it states that this would happen.

It didn't matter to me that others didn't believe in God. I knew what He was doing for me, and I wanted to forever praise Him for that. I was proud of what He'd done for me, and I just wanted to express my appreciation. I was convinced that it had to have been God to make these changes occur in me like this.

Many of the people in my neighborhood finally began to look at me differently. I was told that some people were proud of me, and I was also told that others thought this was just another one of my schemes. Bobby's mother was especially proud of me. I saw her downtown one-day while we both waited for the Metro bus.

"Hi, Jeffrey," she said. "I heard you on the radio one Sunday praying." Sometimes Rev. Brown would let me do the prayer or read a scripture during the Sunday service.

It had been a while since the last time I'd seen Bobby, so I asked her how he was doing.

"Well, son. I'll tell you the truth. Bobby hasn't been doin' nothin' but runnin' the streets. I heard that he is even sellin' drugs on the corner of 23rd Street. Why don't you come by and talk to him? Maybe he'll straighten up," she said.

Bobby's mother was right. He was selling drugs. I was honored that she wanted me to go and speak to him, because it wasn't long ago that she instructed him not to hang out with me, because I was too bad. Now she wants me to go speak to him. Regardless of what doubts others had about my relationship with Christ, Bobby's mother knew I was sincere. That made me feel great.

I told her that I'd be glad to come over and talk to Bobby. "I'll do it tonight."

It was about nine o'clock, and it was dark outside. I didn't want to disappoint Bobby's mother, so I headed around the corner to their house. I was going to try to talk him out of continuing to sell those poisonous drugs.

On the way to their house, I noticed from a distance that there were people scuffling in the streets. It looked like two or three people. I went closer to get a better view. Oh my God! It was two grown men trying to snatch a lady's purse. The lady was holding on to the purse very tightly, but the two thieves were determined to take it away from her.

I stood behind an old house watching this terrible crime take place. It was in my heart to go and help this lady, but I thought I'd just make the situation worse. By my watching this occur, I could be a good eyewitness in court.

The lady must have struggled with them for about ten minutes. She was not going to let go of her purse. One of the thugs then pulled out a pistol. At that time, the lady let the purse go and lied on the ground in the middle of the street and began to cry. The two thieves ran right pass me, but they couldn't see me.

The lady continued to lie there and cry. I felt bad for her and started on my way to help her. As I got near her, she looked up and started to scream.

"I want to help you, ma'am," I pleaded.

But the lady kept shouting hysterically, "Help me! Help me!"

I was petrified and turned to run away. I ran full speed down the alley and didn't stop until I reached Bobby's house. I thought about how this whole situation could be misconstrued, and how I could be charged with this crime. There were no other witnesses. If the lady said that I did this, then most likely I'd be convicted.

That incident was evidence to me that there must be some people who are in prison serving time for something they didn't do. I could've been one. I told Bobby and his mother about the ordeal, and they said that I did the right thing by running.

SECTION III
"Moving In the Spirit"

CHAPTER TWELVE
Through Faith in Jesus

I was becoming more mature on my spiritual journey. I knew that if I wanted to develop a true relationship with God, I must have faith. Faith without works, though, is dead. Although I was a member of an anointed church, I was still faced with a lot of challenges in my neighborhood and at my school.

The challenges in my community mostly came from peers. More of them were indulging in drugs, alcohol and you name it. They'd persistently try to persuade me to join in with them. Thanks to my reading the Bible often, I was aware of their schemes; and, I was not about to accept their wicked ways. Instead, I'd try to get them to do just as I was doing in church. But ministering to the people in my neighborhood was a difficult task. Most of them would counteract what I was saying by telling me that they didn't believe in a God. I'd heard several times, "If there is a God, why does He make it so hard for us black folks?"

Older people usually made that statement. The youth would normally tell me that they didn't want to accept Christ because that would mean that they could no longer party or go out to clubs and stuff. My response to that was "When you accept Christ, it is not that you can't go out to clubs or parties. It is that you will not want to go out to those places."

Rev. Brown would tell us that all the time. We would usually be provided with other things to do to take our minds off of that mess. For instance, the church provided us youth with a lot of extracurricular activities. Rev. Mitchell conducted many of them. Once the church invited us to go to Atlanta, Georgia to visit some of the black colleges there. We went to Morehouse, Spelman, Clark, Morris Brown and Paine College in Augusta, Georgia. The trip was very rewarding and afterwards, I felt that if I did decide to attend college, Paine would be my choice. I had never heard of this school until that trip. I decided on that school because it was located in a small city, and it wasn't congested with thousands of students. Also, I knew that I needed individual attention.

I was blessed to have Rev. Brown pay my way to go on the trip. The cost was fifty dollars. Most of the other youths got money from their parents, but for me, I knew that was impossible. My mother didn't have money like that. She was working only a minimum wage job at Charcoal Steak House. Although she couldn't afford to give me money, she gave me a billion dollars' worth of love.

I was always amazed with Momma. She managed to raise seven kids of her own and five of her younger siblings. I went to my mother one day and asked her how she managed to feed all of us every day, clothe us, and never allow our water, phone, or lights to be turned off. Her only response was, "Through faith in Jesus." It was those words that I vowed to live my life by. I don't know what the future holds, but through faith in Jesus, I know everything will be all right.

It has been almost a year since I was first introduced to the Lord at St. John, and my life has changed tremendously. I no longer have my mischievous urges to steal or fight. Instead, I have the desire to perform well in school. If this is any indication as to what the Lord has in store for my future, I can't wait for it to be revealed. Even though I no longer had those urges, I did begin to develop new ones.

My girlfriend, Alicia, had begun to question me about sex. She'd ask me how I felt about it and if I ever expected to do it with her. I was confused about this whole issue, because although I knew it would be spiritually wrong, I couldn't tell her that. I told her that sex would come in time. I'd been faced with a lot of temptations during my short span as a Christian, but sex was never one, until now.

Alicia and I began to spend every day together in school. We had a secret meeting place in the upstairs gym. It was there that we'd kiss and hold each other. We'd only do this between classes because she wasn't allowed to date. Alicia had given me a different perspective on life. She was the perfect looking girl-- dark-skinned, pretty face and long legs. Not only that, she was popular.

It was through her that I made a lot of new friends. One in particular was named Fred Garrett. Hank was his nickname. Hank was a nice guy. We seemed to kick it off from the beginning. I guess we became good friends because we both had similar interests. For one, he was preparing to run track for the school in the spring, and he also attended the Kingdom Hall regularly.

One thing we didn't have in common was our looks. Hank was a handsome ladies' man. He used to tell me that girls usually just liked him because of his outgoing personality. That could've been true, because he was very outgoing. He'd always be smiling and joking around. But that was not the only reason girls liked him a lot. Hank was a good dresser, and he kept his hair very neat. He had so many waves in his hair that I would tease him by saying that he was making me seasick.

Almost every day, Alicia, Hank and I would eat after school at McDonald's across the street. This one day we went there, we had a great time. However, upon leaving, it was discovered that Alicia's purse was missing.

"Somebody stole my purse," she said. She kept asking if any of us had seen it. "Not me," I said. "Honey, I don't even remember you bringing your purse." "Well, I did, and I know I did," she said as she stormed out of the door and into her car.

"Alicia, hey," I said as I went after her. She was so upset that she just rushed to

her car and slammed the door before I could reach her. I was baffled by her behavior. It seemed that she was upset with me. Before I could ask her, she drove off down the street.

Hank and I discussed this matter afterwards. He said that she was probably rushing to get home in order to call the banks so that she could cancel her checks and credit cards.

"You're right," I said. "I'll just call her later to see how it went."

That evening, I phoned Alicia several times. Each time I'd call her little sister said that she wasn't home. I didn't understand what was actually happening. How could the girl I love, the only girl that I loved like this, now be so upset with me? Maybe she thought that I made her lose her purse, or maybe she just felt that if she hadn't met me, she wouldn't have been in the restaurant in the first place. Anyway, three days had gone by, and I still didn't hear anything from Alicia. Then, Hank called me.

"What's up, Jeff? Guess what, man? I know why Alicia hasn't been talkin' to you."

"You do? Please tell me, man."

"Well, Jeff, she believes that you stole her purse," said Hank.

"No, you lyin'," I said in a frustrated voice. "I told her that I didn't steal anymore.

I told her that I have committed my life to Christ. I'm not like that anymore." Hank quietly listened to what I said, and when I finished, he paused before he said what he had to say.

"Well, brother, I'm just telling you what I heard. I was told that she said that you were once a thief. It is all over school that you stole her purse."

I knew that what Hank was telling me was true, because Jake called me after Hank did to tell me the same thing. Both Jake and Hank knew I was innocent, and they both admitted feeling bad that this was happening to me. Some people didn't believe me. Tuffy was one of those people.

The next day I was hesitant about going to school. I felt bad about this whole ordeal. How could she possibly think that I had stolen her purse? I saw Tuffy that morning as I waited to catch the bus to school. He approached me with one of those "you need to be ashamed of yourself" looks on his face.

"Hey, Tuffy, what you doin' out here on the corner so early in the mornin'?" I asked him.

"Well, brother. I got to make my money. I got to get paid. I found me a new group of people to sell these drugs to."

"Oh, yeah? Who's that?"

"School kids," he said. "The kids do this stuff like it's goin' outta style." "Brother, you need to be ashamed of yourself. That's absolutely ridiculous. Don't you know it's hard enough for our people to survive without you sellin' that poison to them?" I said.

"Yeah, I know, man, but, hell. They gon' get it, anyway, so why not let it be from me. Anyway, Jeffrey, you got me into this. You got me into this wantin' to

make-money-fast thing. Remember? Let's steal this. Let's steal that," he said sarcastically.

"I didn't get you into drugs, brother, so please don't say that. By the way, if you want to do what I do, why don't you let all that go and come to church with me?"

"Hell, no! I don't believe in that stuff." By this time the bus was coming. "Okay, Tuffy. I'll be praying for you," I said before I stepped on the bus.

"No, fool, you don't have to pray for me. I'm going to pray for you. You're the one who's goin' around stealin' purses. Yeah, I heard about it," he laughed, as the bus doors closed.

I can't believe this. Even Tuffy heard about it, and he only comes to school once a week. This is crazy! How can they believe I stole her purse? Had it been a year or two ago they may have been right, but not now. I'm trying to do the right thing.

For the next couple of days, I tried to find comfort by reading the Bible. I needed to get my mind off of this false accusation. The word of God helped me a lot. It was there that I read that even Jesus himself was unjustly accused.

Things began to die down after a couple of weeks, and I finally began to forget about the incident. During that time, I only saw Alicia in passing. She still refused to speak to me, but that was okay. I was used to it by now.

It was later revealed that Alicia's purse was not stolen after all. What happened was that she left her purse in her father's old car the day before we went to McDonald's. Her father's car had broken down that same day and it was in the shop for a whole month. It wasn't until the car was returned that this mistake was discovered. In spite of her having found her purse, she still refused to speak to me. She didn't even say she was sorry. I guess she was too embarrassed. At any rate, I forgave her and wished her well.

CHAPTER THIRTEEN
Being Rewarded for Doing The Right Thing

"The wicked man earns deceptive wages, but he who sows righteousness reaps a sure reward." Proverbs 11:18 (NIV)

I enjoyed praising the Lord. There was a certain sense of comfort that came over me. My financial situation had not changed, meaning we were still poor. I now, though, felt rich inside. I would pray often, and when able, I'd try to get others to pray with me. I can recall once when I went by Bobby's house, he had just finished arguing with his mother.

"Hey, Bobby. What's wrong, man?"

"Well, she just gettin' on my nerves again."

I then asked him where he was going, although I knew that there was a ninety percent chance that he was going on the corner of 23rd Street to hang out with the vagabonds of the neighborhood to drink cheap liquor and sell nickel bags of reefer.

"What do you mean, where am I goin'? You know where I'm goin.'"

"Bobby, I don't understand, brother. You got a lot goin' for you. Man, you're not like the rest of them. You used to go to church. You said you were saved. You know that there is a God, and that He loves you. So, why do you waste your time on that corner?"

Bobby looked at me like I was crazy. I got the feeling that he was tired of me preaching to him.

"Look, I know all that, man, and I don't feel like hearing it, okay?"

"No, it ain't okay. I remember when I was out trying to steal everything I could, and you'd tell me that I needed to get right. Now, I'm tellin' you . . ."

"Yeah, yeah, yeah. That was then, this is now. I got tired of that, man. It's like I'd try hard to accept God, but what I saw made it hard for me," he said.

"What did you see?" I asked.

"Well, for one, do you remember that one minister at my church, Rev. Henderson?"

"Yeah, I remember."

"Well, he used to come to church preachin' to us about doin' right, and all along, he was just as crooked as he wanna be."

"What do you mean?"

"Okay, Jeffrey. Since I can trust you, I'm gonna tell you. Just promise not to tell anyone. One day when I was asked by Rev. Henderson to stay after church in order to help him move some furniture, he . . ." Before Bobby continued to tell the story, he looked at me with the eyes of an innocent child. It was like he thought I would be disappointed in him or something.

"What happened, brother? Just relax," I said.

"Well, after I helped him move the furniture, he . . . he . . . Well, . . . you see. We were the only ones left in the church, and at first, I couldn't believe what he was tryin' to do, but he tried to hit on me."

"What? You're kiddin'? How?"

"What do you mean how? He tried to hit on me the same way we'd hit on a girl."

He is a faggot. Bobby tried to smile a little when he told me this, but I knew that his smile was simply a barricade hiding the hurt and disappointment that he really felt.

I wanted to offer some advice. I was asking God to please give me something to say. I had never been faced with a situation like this before, and I guess because of the shock of the news I'd just heard, I couldn't bring myself to utter one word. Instead, I stood there, staring at Bobby as if I saw a ghost. I was speechless.

It felt as though we had been standing there for several minutes. Bobby then turned and walked away. How could this be true? Rev. Henderson is a well-known preacher in our city. Why would he . . .? How . . .? Lord, I pray that You please give me an understanding.

I prayed over and over for Bobby. I went to visit him as often as possible in order to get him to realize that Rev. Henderson was not God, and that God has all power. It is He whom we need to focus on. I also asked Bobby not to give up on church altogether because of this, but to come and join our church. Bobby said he'd give it some thought. But, two days later, I saw him and Tuffy on the corner selling drugs as usual. Bobby just said hi and acted as if he'd completely forgotten our last conversation.

Making quick money was always the objective in the minds of the youths in our 'hood. It had always been like that. I wasn't surprised, because I, too, thought the same way a while ago. Now I don't focus much on what I don't have. I focus on what I do have a new opportunity to live my life; this time for Christ. I'm thankful for my health and my family. I'm just thankful to know Christ like I do. I realize that it could be me on the corner or in the alley doing drugs. It could be me in jail or dead like many of my friends. In fact, one friend of mine was killed just the other day.

The police shot him. The police said that he drew a gun on them when they interfered with him burglarizing a house. I don't believe the police's statement because I knew the alleged burglar. I knew him well. We graduated from middle school together. I know that he had sense enough not to pull a gun on "the man." Anyway, it didn't matter now, because he was dead. Incidents like this happened all the time.

I had no desire to make money illegally. I did pray to God that He'd at least make it possible for me to earn some money, the right way. As a senior in high school, there were a lot of things that I wanted to buy a class ring, scrapbook, yearbook, etc. I knew that the Lord would make a way for me.

One night, while I was home spending time with my family, the phone rang. It was State Representative Bill Smith. Mr. Smith was a member of our church and a well-liked politician in our city. He indicated to me that his purpose for calling was because he heard that I was a good artist. Someone must have told him that I was enrolled in Performing Arts class. It may have been his daughter. She attended Broad Ripple, and she, too, was a member of our church.

"Yes, sir, I can draw pretty well," I said.

"I have this project you may be interested in," he said. "We are working on a new campaign called, "People Against Crime." P A C. for short. Anyway, we want you to draw a logo for us, and we'll gladly pay you."

I told him without hesitation that I'd gladly draw the logo. The logo they had in mind would be a PacMan (from the video game) eating a burglar. This was a popular video game. Mr. Smith asked if I could have the logo ready by tomorrow evening, because he needed to present it to the group by then.

By the evening of the next day, I had drawn three different logos. Mr. Smith only saw the first one and said that he liked it.

"I'll take this one," he said. "I don't need to see anymore. This is fine."

It took me less than fifteen minutes to draw that particular logo. I was given seventy-five dollars for my work. Seventy-five dollars for fifteen minutes of work! This is great! Not only was I given that money, but I was told that the logo would be placed on buttons to be issued to all of the public high schools in Indianapolis.

I felt great. Last year I was selling stolen goods and wasn't making this kind of money. Now, I'm serving God, and He has allowed me to make more money using a talent that I already had-- an honest talent drawing.

"He shall call upon me, and I will answer him: I will be with him in trouble. I will deliver him and honor him." Psalm 91:15 (KJV)

I didn't care what happened from there. I wasn't going to let anything interfere with my love for Christ. I know He answers prayers.

Once the buttons were distributed to all the public schools, several other adults heard about me and my gift of drawing. They, too, gave me jobs to do. For a while, I was getting more orders than I could fill. A lady on the usher board asked me to do something for her husband. A lady at school and even Rev. Brown gave me jobs. Rev. Brown asked me to draw a picture of Dr. Martin Luther King, Jr. in order for it to be placed in the church's newsletter, since it was close to Dr. King's birthday. It took me forty minutes to draw the picture of Dr. King, and Rev. Brown gave me one hundred dollars for my work. Thank you, Jesus! I was making more money being honest than I did as a thief. "So do not throw away your confidence; it will be richly rewarded. You need to persevere so that when you have done the will of God, you will receive what he has promised." Hebrews 10:35,36 (NIV).

CHAPTER FOURTEEN
The Best Mental Attitude Award

I can't believe it! It is now close to graduation time, and I was told that I would definitely be one of the lucky students marching this year. At the beginning of the year, my school counselor told me that it was doubtful that I'd graduate this year due to my first two years of terrible grades at Manual. However, she told me that if I worked hard, it would be possible. Well, I worked hard. On June 7, I will be graduating from Broad Ripple School of Performing Arts.

Hank and I were looking forward to graduation. We had been spending a lot of time together and had become the best of friends. Our friendship strengthened towards the end of the school year due to us being on the track team. We were on the mile relay team and competed in the 400-meter dash together. We were two of the fastest runners on the team and had a true love for the sport. We practiced together every other day. I'd usually meet him over at his house and from there we'd jog five miles downtown. I had always loved to run track, even at Manual, but my negative attitude prevented me from having the opportunity to be a part of the team. Now, not only was I a part of the team, I was an outstanding athlete. In fact, during our end of the season banquet, I was the recipient of the Outstanding Athlete Award and the award that surprised me most of all, the Best Mental Attitude Award.

Accepting Christ and doing His will have really paid off in my life. I was so thrilled at what I knew God could do. I made a vow to one day go back into my community and spread the message of peace so that one day those young people who are lost could find and accept God. They too can realize the joy that I have.

I knew that there was hope for all of our people regardless of their circumstances, and I prayed that the Lord would use me as a tool to help them realize that there is hope. It is that thought that triggered me to really think seriously about college. Before then, I didn't really have a strong desire to attend. Because of this new perspective on higher education, I prayed once again to make this dream become a reality. I knew that if I got accepted to anybody's college, it would have to be through a miracle. I'm glad that I know God works miracles.

I was advised, however, that due to my poor grades, it would be necessary for me to take the SAT. I knew that I had to score at least a thousand. I registered for the test and in two weeks I was to take it. Hank, Jake, and I were studying every day after school. I hadn't taken too many standardized tests, and I dreaded having to take this one.

One of my motivating forces for really wanting to do well on this test was that I knew that if I went to college and graduated, I would make my mother really happy. You see, no one in my family had graduated from a four-year college. Another source of inspiration was if by some miracle I did graduate, it would allow others to really see how the Lord had transformed my life. Right now, it was too early for me to dream of graduating from college. I first needed to conquer this test.

The day of taking the big test had arrived. As I entered the cafeteria where the test was being administered, I saw Jake and Hank sitting together in the rear of the room. I wanted to join them, but there weren't any empty seats. Therefore, I sat across the room and took my test. It seemed as though those questions would never end. They eventually did.

In retrospect, the test was kind of simple. That could be because I skipped the ones that I didn't know and did what I could. Both Jake and Hank seemed satisfied with their test performances. Now all we could do was wait for our results.

Meanwhile, at the church, Rev. Brown had arranged for us youth to attend a retreat. It was to take place somewhere called Fox Lake. I had never been on a retreat and didn't know what it was until Jake told me that it was like camping. I liked camping, so now, I was looking forward to going.

I was excited on the day that we were to leave. A few months earlier, I had gone to the dentist and had a partial tooth placed in my mouth. Now the missing tooth that was knocked out during my freshman year at Manual was replaced.

When my tooth was missing, I really didn't appreciate my looks. There were times when I'd hate to look in the mirror. Before I lost my tooth, I was the life of the party always joking. While it was gone, I would only speak occasionally, and that was mostly in church. Now those days of shunning from myself in the mirror were over. I'm going to talk as often as possible, and it couldn't have happened at a better time. Many of my friends from church didn't even realize that my tooth had been replaced.

During the retreat, we had a good time. We were lodging in cabins, and between discussing church related issues, we'd play softball in an open field or go swimming.

Once when I went swimming, Jake and I, along with a couple of girls were jumping around, slamming each other in the water. At one point, Jake grabbed me from behind. As I was trying to get away from him, my tooth fell out of my mouth. The water that we were playing in was actually a dark lake. Therefore, as my tooth fell, I couldn't see where it landed.

I wanted to retrieve that tooth so badly that Jake and I spent the rest of the evening trying to locate it. We had been hunting for it so long that we had to leave the water because the pool was closing. I was very upset that I'd lost my tooth. The tooth had cost me a lot of money that I had been saving for some time. Now it was gone. How can I face the group without my front tooth? This was devastating to me. I decided not to go to the youth meeting that evening. Instead, I went to Rev. Mitchell's room. He always seemed to know what to say to uplift my spirit.

"Hello, Rev. Mitchell," I said as I entered his room. I didn't have to say much to him in order for him to know something was wrong.

"What's the problem, Jeffrey?" he asked. I told him about my situation, and to my surprise he chuckled.

"What's funny?" I said. "How could you giggle at my tragedy?"

"I thought something was wrong. Jeffrey, you've overcome a lot of things. You were headed for hell in a hand basket. Now you're saved. Do you know what being saved means?"

Before I could respond Rev. Mitchell continued to speak. "Being saved means that you now have accepted Christ into your life. The body of Christ lives in you. That's a wonderful thing, Jeffrey. That is the greatest thing you could ask for. But, guess what, Jeffrey?" he asked as his expression became more serious.

"Your being saved is not great for everybody, especially, Satan. Satan will come and try to steal your joy. He'll try to steal your Jesus from inside of you. You see, Satan knew that you invested a lot in that tooth. He knew you were excited about having it. Therefore, he knew that if he took it, he could also take your joy."

Rev. Mitchell continued to preach to me. It was as if each of his words was making my disappointment lighter. I was beginning to realize that a tooth is a tooth. Satan can have that, but I won't let him have me.

Rev. Mitchell concluded by saying, "You must resist the devil, and he'll flee from you (James 4:7). Deal aggressively with Satan in Jesus' name. Exercise the authority you have through His name, His shed blood, and word of God (Luke 10:19). The devil has a lot of schemes to make you upset, mad, or just simply frustrated, and when he does that, he takes you away from focusing on God's word. Don't let your missing tooth be the devil's scheme."

"Put on the full armor of God so that you can take your stand against the devil's schemes." Ephesians 6:11 (NIV)

Rev. Mitchell's consultation helped me a lot. After I left his room, I rushed to the meeting room to join my fellow Christian youth brothers and sisters. During the meeting, I was talking so much that Jake offered me money to shut up.

When I returned home from the retreat, my mother was there waiting.

"I have something for you, son," she said. As she approached me, she handed me an envelope. It contained my SAT scores. I hurriedly opened the letter. I hope that I've gotten the score needed to go to college.

I opened the letter, and to my surprise, it wasn't a thousand. It wasn't even close to a thousand. I did awful. Graduation was not far away, and I did horribly.

When Jake and Hank asked me what my score was, I refused to tell them. However, I did tell them that I was still going to college. I told everyone that I was going. I know that my school transcript shows that my grades are poor and that my SAT score is sad, but I'm still going to go. It was revealed to me just like it was revealed to me that I was going to transfer to Broad Ripple School of Performing Arts. I constantly prayed that it would happen.

"I'll do anything, God. Just allow me to go to college," I'd pray. I had become weary in regard to what I needed to do in order to take the first steps in pursuing this dream. Therefore, I tried to contact Ricky Johnson, a friend of mine from my old school. Ricky and I hadn't seen each other in a long time since I transferred schools. I knew he was smart and could direct me with answers about college.

I couldn't reach him by phone, so I made plans to go to Ricky's house, but before I had the chance to go, I saw him at Douglas Park during the Indiana Black Expo festivities, an event that brought together various artists and speakers.

"Hey, Ricky," I said as we shook hands and hugged each other.

Ricky was a pleasant person to be around. He was always that way. He had a slender build and stood about six feet tall. Most of the times I would see Ricky, he'd be by himself. Once when I asked him why this was, he stated that he liked being alone because most of the people he knew stayed in trouble, and he didn't want any parts of trouble. I told him that I had been looking for him, and that it was a blessing to meet this way.

"What? You've been lookin' for me?" he asked. "Yeah, man. I wanted to ask you about college."

"College? The last time I saw you, you weren't thinkin' about college. What is Do you need information for someone else?" "No," I replied.

I then began to explain to him the spiritual transformation that occurred in my life. Once I'd done this, he looked at me with disbelief. However, he asked me to come by his house, and he'd explain all that I needed to know.

A couple of days had passed before I decided to go by Ricky's house. Hank went along with me since after all, he was doing the driving. Hank would usually drive his father's brand new Sedan de Ville Cadillac, and he always kept it clean.

When we arrived at Ricky's house, I introduced Hank to him. We sat around and talked about everything under the sun before we began to discuss my going to college. I explained my desire to attend a small college in Augusta, Georgia called Paine College. Ricky indicated that because of my poor high school transcript, as well as my poor SAT score, it would be best for me to send the college a personal letter explaining my situation and to contact them by phone in order to speak with the Director of Admissions.

I did just that. Not only did I send a letter, but I also asked my pastor to send one. When I called, I spoke to a man named Mr. Lewis, who was the Director of Admissions. Mr. Lewis was impressed with my desire to attend Paine College, but he recommended that I try to enroll in a trade school due to my grades. I didn't want to enroll in a trade school. I wanted to enroll in Paine College.

This is what I prayed about. This is what the Lord revealed to me. I will go to college. I don't care what Mr. Lewis said, because I God told me.

CHAPTER FIFTEEN
God's Voice

It was finally time to graduate from Broad Ripple. Hank and I had been hanging together all week long. We had been together basically every minute of the day. I even spent the night at his house. I slept in the bed that was in the basement. His mother and father were extremely nice, and they welcomed me. I considered Hank's family as the perfect one. He had a mother and a father. They lived in the same house, and they appeared to always be happy. Hank also had two younger brothers named Derrick and Kevin.

During this time, I was spending more time at their house than my own. There were times when Hank would come to my house, but I made sure that those times were few, and that he didn't stay long. I was embarrassed for him to come to my house because of its appearance and the fact that it was not in a good neighborhood like theirs.

The commencement ceremony was fun, but it was the after party that I enjoyed most. In fact, this must have been the most fun that I ever had. It was held at the YMCA. We were dancing, swimming, playing basketball doing everything.

The following day, Ricky, Hank and I got together and discussed our futures. Ricky stated that for now, he just wanted a job. Hank was undecided. As for me, I still wanted to go to college, Paine College. I knew that I needed to continue to learn. Even though my last year of high school was full of good grades, I still felt ignorant when it came to a lot of things.

"Jeffrey, have you heard from Paine?" Ricky asked. "No, I haven't," I said.

By this time, I had sent two letters to the college, but I hadn't gotten a formal reply yet. Two weeks had gone by before I did.

Pat brought me a letter that was mailed from Paine College. The letter had been opened already. My mother must have opened it, as she did most of my mail. I wondered why Momma didn't tell me what the letter said. It must have been bad news. It was. The letter stated that because of my grades in high school and my low SAT scores, I could not be accepted to the college. It was a denial letter. I couldn't believe it. I knew that my first two years of high school were bad, but they should have at least given me a chance. They knew by my last year that I was at least trying.

I heard God's voice again telling me not to worry. He told me that I would go. So why should I worry? With that thought in mind I got excited again. Forget the letter. I'm going to college. My spirit felt relieved, and my mind was confident. It was so confident that I once again went around to all my friends and told them that in August I would be leaving Indianapolis, Indiana to go to Augusta, Georgia.

I saw Jake in the game room.

"Hey, Jake. You know I'm leavin' for college in August." I saw Hank in the market.

"Hank, I'm outta here in August, brother." "So did you get accepted?" Hank asked.

"No, I didn't get accepted really, but I know I'm still goin.'" "Okay, Jeffrey, whatever you say."

Then I saw Tuffy. He was in the parking lot of the McDonald's on 38th and Illinois. He was driving a brand new car. A car that I knew he must have bought with his drug money.

"Tuffy, hey, is this your car?"

"Hell, yeah, it's my car. Who else's?"

"Well, all I want to tell you is that I'll be leavin' here in August to go to college." "What? Man, you crazy. What are you goin' to college for? All you gon' end up

doin' is workin' for the white man, and he ain't gon' pay you nothin'. You won't ever be able to have this," he said as he pulled out a wad of money and pointed to it.

"That's all right, Tuffy. I don't need that. I have somethin' better." Before I could say anything else Tuffy stopped me.

"Oh boy. Here he goes with that God stuff again. It's time to go." He then got in his car and took off. As he left, I stood there for a moment and watched as he sped down the street. God help him. I'd always say a prayer for Tuffy, because I still felt responsible for what he was doing.

In the meantime, Jake, Hank, Ricky, and I were having a great time being friends. For the most part, we would go to the park every evening and talk about girls, basketball and whatever else came to mind. We had the best time just joking around with each other. We were always playing jokes on one another. One afternoon, Ricky, Hank, and me went to Jake's house. His mother invited us in and directed us to his bedroom where he was fast asleep.

"Let's scare him," said Hank.

"Yeah, let me do it," said Ricky. At that moment Ricky ran out to his car to get an old spooky mask that he had there since last Halloween. He put the mask on, then kneeled beside the bed where Jake was sleeping.

"Cut the lights off," Hank said.

The room was almost completely dark. The only thing that you could see was a streak of light that shined on the mask that Ricky had now put on. We knew that Jake was scared of everything anyway, therefore we knew that this joke would work.

Ricky reached over to tap Jake on the shoulder to wake him. Before he could tap him, Hank couldn't hold his laugh in, so he started laughing hysterically. At that time, Jake opened his eyes. Once he saw the mask he yelled like crazy. He yelled so loud that he scared us too. We all then ran out of the room laughing. It worked!

Jake was so scared that he continued to scream for at least another minute or two after we left.

"What's goin' on?" Jake asked. After he caught on to what was happening, he began to laugh. "I'm gonna get y'all back. Believe me."

I really had fun with my friends. However, I knew that it would only be a matter of time before I would be leaving for college. I was looking forward to college, but I wasn't looking forward to leaving my friends. They were the only friends I ever had who weren't interested in stealing, doing drugs or committing crimes. I thanked God for Jake, Ricky and Hank.

Paine College was to begin its fall semester in one week. I had sent two more letters to the school requesting them to reconsider and allow me to enroll this fall. I had also made several more calls to Mr. Lewis, but at this point, I still have yet to hear anything different.

"Jeffrey, you still goin' to college?" said Hank. "Yeah, I'm goin'," I said.

"Well, school will be startin' soon, and it don't look like you're preparin' yourself to go nowhere," Ricky said.

"Look, fellas. I told y'all I'm goin' to college, and I'm goin'," I told them in a frustrated tone of voice.

Even though I was sure that the voice that I heard telling me that I was going to college came from God, I began to question if I would be going this fall. I have to go! I told everyone that I was going, and I'd really be disappointed if I didn't.

Today was August the 12th. Paine College freshmen began enrolling on the 10th, and I haven't heard anything. What was I to do? It looked as if my dream to attend college was not coming true. I began to pray. After I prayed, I felt the need to fast for a day. I felt that if I fasted, it would show my loyalty to Christ and allow Him to see how sincere I was and how bad I wanted to go to college. The day after I fasted, I got on my knees to pray again. This time in the middle of my prayer a voice told me to call Mr.

Lewis. The voice was very clear, and I knew that it was what I needed to do.

It was five o'clock in the evening, and it's possible that the college was closed for the day. However, that didn't stop me. I picked up the phone and made the long distance call to Augusta. The phone rang several times before someone finally picked it up.

"Hello. May I speak to Mr. Lewis?"

"Let me see if he's still here," the voice said from the other end. "You're in luck.

He is here. I'll transfer you to his office."

He picked up the phone, and before I could explain who I was he interrupted me. "Yes, I know who you are. How are you doing, Jeffrey? We were just talking about you, the Dean of Academic Affairs, Mr. Williams, and me. I told Mr. Williams of your interest in our school and for the last twenty minutes we have been discussing how we can handle this situation. You called at a perfect time, Jeffrey.

"What we came up with is this. Since your grades are poor, it is next to impossible to accept you in the regular class. But what we can do is enroll you in what we call Help Courses. These courses will prepare you for our regular classes. If you pass, you'll be accepted into the regular classes and can then begin on the road to

commencement. However, I must tell you that if you fail these courses your enrollment in the school will be terminated."

"So, what you're sayin' is I can come to Paine College?" I asked. "Yes," he said.

At that moment, I felt chills travel through my body. "Thank you, Jesus!" I said.

Once again, the Lord made a way for me. He told me that in order for me to register for the fall semester, I must be at the school the following day. Ironically, my suitcase was already packed. I left for Paine that night.

Less than six hours after I spoke to Mr. Lewis I was on my way via Greyhound to Augusta, Georgia. I had to leave so quickly that I didn't even have a chance to bid farewell to Jake, Hank, and Ricky. I did, however, say goodbye to my family. My mother was so proud of me that she cried as I boarded the bus.

I had never been away from home by myself before for a long period of time. I had never even left the state by myself. Therefore, I must admit, I was frightened. I had been so anxious and excited about going to college that I didn't have a chance to be afraid. But now it hit me. I was on this big quiet bus with total strangers headed for a place I knew hardly anything about. What will it be like? Who will I meet there? Will they like me? Many thoughts entered my mind. I didn't know what to think. I was afraid. Suddenly, the thought of me growing up was finally hitting me. Now there will be no mother to console in, no brothers and sisters to visit, no Jake, Hank, and Ricky to hang out with. For a moment, I felt like going back home. No way, I have to be a man. I have to grow up.

"We'll be in Augusta, Georgia in fifteen minutes," said the bus driver. I was awakened by his voice over the intercom.

"This is it," I said as I looked out of the window as the bus pulled into the Augusta bus terminal. The city looked smaller than I remembered it from the day that the church brought us here to visit. It was six o'clock in the morning, and I guess that's why there weren't many cars on the road. All I saw as I stood in front of the terminal waiting on a taxi were old houses and used car lots. I can't believe it! I'm finally here. I'm going to college! This is what I prayed for, and the Lord did His part. Now it's time for me to do mine. From that point on I was determined to do my best. "Hey, taxi! Take me to Paine College."

When I arrived at the campus, I noticed that it was very small, but clean.

"Can you direct me to Epworth Hall?" I asked a female student as she was exiting.

When I entered Epworth Hall, I was approached by Mr. Gulley. He was the resident director. He informed me of all I needed to know. He then directed me to my room, Room #201. Before I entered the room, I stood in front of the door wondering. Who will be my roommate? Will he be a drunk, a smoker, a person who liked drugs or a thug who might try to entice me into mischief? I had no idea. Because of this I once again became weary, weary of who stood on the other side of that door. I pray that whoever it is, Lord, allow us to get along.

I then opened the door. When I did, I saw a young man sitting in front of a desk reading. He was a light skinned young man with a clean cut. He was dressed in a suit and tie, and he welcomed me with a bright smile.

"Hi, my name is Jeffrey Thomas. I'm from Indianapolis, Indiana," I said as I reached out my hand to him.

"Hello," he said. "I'm from a small town called Washington, Georgia. By the way, this town was the first town named after our founding father." He then began to laugh. "Oh, forgive me for being rude. My name is Reverend Sam Anderson."

"Reverend!" I said excitedly.

He looked quite young to be a reverend, but as I looked on his desk and saw all of the biblical literature, I knew he was serious. This was a true blessing. Out of all the people I could've ended up with as a roommate, I got a preacher. Thank you, Jesus!

Rev. Anderson and I became instant friends. His being a reverend didn't stop him from expressing his great sense of humor. We became such good friends that I started calling him Rev. Rev and I had an affinity for just having a good time. Therefore, a lot of times after class, we would hang out on campus and play football and other games with the students. It wasn't long before we began to meet other guys and include them in our close circuit of friends. There came Modou Bendou from Africa, Carlton Mansey from Atlanta, Ken Nance from Augusta, Henry Davis from Millen, Georgia and Jack Rosier from Dublin, Georgia. I had friends from all over the globe. We all enjoyed hanging together, and on Sundays, we'd go to church.

I was glad that we all got along, but I felt kind of inferior intellectually. You see Modou was valedictorian of his high school class. Rev was his senior class president. Henry seemed pretty smart, and look at me? My grades were so poor that I had to come to college on a negotiation. Once again, I became weary. Will I be able to cut the mustard? Or will I simply flunk my classes and be sent back home to Indiana? I didn't know what my future held, but with that thought I was reminded of an old gospel song "I Don't Believe He Brought Me this Far to Leave Me."

CHAPTER SIXTEEN
Like a Thief, a Thief, a Thief in The Night

Now six weeks had gone by since I'd been at Paine. My life was going better than I could have ever imagined. Not only was I doing well in my courses, but also, I joined the track team, and I was recently hired to work at this fancy restaurant. Since my schedule was now so busy, the time that I spent with Rev and the fellas was limited.

However, at night, we would all still find time to get together and pray. Rev made it a point that we all prayed together every night, regardless of what else we were doing. Most of the time, Rev would do the prayer, but for some reason this particular day, I expressed the need to do it. When I prayed, I asked Jesus to bless all of my friends the new ones and the ones in Indianapolis. I felt the unusual urge to pray for my friends back home. After the prayer, Rev looked at me and asked what was wrong. He said I prayed like I had something on my mind.

"Nothin' is wrong," I said. "I just felt like prayin.'"

Early the next morning, before anyone got up, I laid in my bed wide-awake. I couldn't sleep for some reason. Then I heard the phone ring down the hall. There was only one phone on each hall-- one phone for every forty men. I'd hear the phone ring all the time, so it wasn't a big deal. But, this time, for some strange reason, I felt the phone was for me.

"Jeffrey Thomas!" someone yelled from way down the hall. "Come get the phone!"

It was a little after six o'clock in the morning. Who and why would anybody be calling me this early? It must be bad news.

I slowly walked down the hall where the phone was. As I picked it up, I heard Jake's voice on the other end.

"Hey, man, what's up?" I asked.

Jake paused before he said anything else.

"I got bad news," he said.

I didn't want to ask him what was wrong, but I knew it was just a matter of time before I would find out.

"What happened?" I asked him. "Well . . . Mookey got killed."

Mookey was a boy I grew up with. He was three years younger than I was and he always considered me his big brother. I met him when I was eight and he was five. We lived down the alley from each other. The last time that I saw Mookey was the day before I left to come to college.

He drove his new car over to my house and asked me for advice on fixing it up. The car he bought was a big nineteen seventy-six, four door Buick. The body of the car was in good shape, but the inside needed some serious work. I referred him to a place to have the work done.

Mookey's death was a big shock to me because he was only sixteen years old. I remember when he was six years old. We were playing cops and robbers in my yard. Once we finished playing, we were so exhausted that we sat down on the steps in front of my house. While sitting there we began to talk about death.

"What is death?" Mookey asked.

"Death is when you leave this world and never come back," I said.

I noticed that Mookey became quiet. I looked over at him. He was crying. "What's wrong with you?" I asked him.

"I don't want to die."

"Awe, man, be quiet. People don't die until they get old."

At that point, Mookey and I changed subjects and continued playing cops and robbers.

"Jeffrey, Jeffrey, you all, right?" Jake said from the other end of the phone. "Yes, I'm all right, brother, but tell me. How did he die?"

"Well, he and some friends were gamblin' in the alley behind 26th and College and an argument started, and Mookey was shot in the chest with a double barrel," Jake said.

Mookey's death had a serious effect on me. It made me appreciate my life more, and it strengthened my desire to want to go back to my community and assist the youth with doing better for themselves. The thing that happened to Mookey happened all the time in the black community. If we don't get serious about administering proper guidance to our black youth, then this will continue to happen. I feel that each person's life is very, very important, and I'm going to devote my life to getting others to realize this too. I owe this to Mookey.

The next day I went to my counselor's office and told her that I wanted to major in Criminology/Sociology.

"Let your light so shine before men, that they may see your good works, and glorify your Father which is in heaven." Matthew 5:16 (KJV)

Rev and the rest of my friends in college knew that I was upset about Mookey's death, and they did their best to cheer me up. It was then that I explained to them my past. We must have talked for three hours about this, because they kept asking me questions. Rev asked the most questions. I guess since he was from a small town, he couldn't relate to what I was saying.

Not only did I explain my past, but I also told them what I wanted to do in the future.

"I want to get a degree from here, and then go back into my old neighborhood and teach the young people, particularly males, about how to respect themselves, how to appreciate life, and most of all, how important it is to love and follow the practices of Jesus Christ."

I then explained to them about the movie I saw long ago with Pat Boone, and how he went into the gang community and struggled with the youths until he got them to accept the word of God. I am thoroughly convinced that that is the only way to really reach our dying community.

The first semester was coming to an end. I passed all of my Help Courses. It looked like I would be returning the following semester. I decided to go back home for the Christmas holidays. I again caught the Greyhound bus and headed home. This was a much better trip because I couldn't wait to see everyone.

After greeting my family and telling them how much I enjoyed college, I hurriedly went to meet Hank, Jake, and Ricky. We all met up at Hank's house. Hank's parents were gone out of town for the holidays. The fellas were happy to see me, especially Hank. He jumped on my back. They all joked about how I left for college so fast that I didn't say goodbye.

The weather was getting very bad. The weatherman announced that we would have a blizzard. We decided to go to the grocery store down the street in order to stock up and return to Hank's house in case we couldn't get back home during the blizzard. We all lived at least a mile away from Hank. We decided to spend the night at Hank's house since his parents were gone.

We knew that it was important to buy nutritious, healthy foods since we may be trapped inside for a couple of days. Therefore, we bought two gallons of ice cream, several packs of cookies, sodas, and potato chips.

Sure, enough a blizzard did come. It was a bad one too. I looked out of the window and saw nothing but white snow blowing fast. The blizzard lasted for several days, and those days were truly some of the best that I ever had. They were fun because during that time, all we did was look at movies, play board games, wrestle, play music, and call our other friends on the phone. It had been a long time since I had a genuinely good time with those guys.

The holiday break had gone by too quickly. It was now time to go back to Augusta. On the day that I was to leave, Hank drove me to the Greyhound bus station. During this drive, we had a serious conversation.

"Tell me Hank. Did you see Mookey before he died?" I asked. "Yeah, I saw him all the time."

"Well, did you go to the funeral?"

"No, I don't like to go to funerals, man."

We finally arrived at the bus terminal. I got there just in time, because the people were lining up in line number four to Atlanta, the line I needed to be in. I would catch the bus to Atlanta and transfer to Augusta from there.

Hank waited with me. As I stepped closer to enter the bus, Hank said, "Hey, man. When you get back in the summer, I'm gonna have a surprise for you. I met this girl who thinks you are cute. She's a friend of my girl's, and I'm gonna introduce y'all when you get back."

"Okay, Hank. I would appreciate that. I won't be back home until spring break."

At that point, we both waved goodbye and I mentally prepared myself for this long eighteen-hour bus ride.

It had been six weeks since the spring semester started. I had my new classes, and I was doing well in them. Spring break would be in two weeks, but for some reason, I wasn't as excited about this break as I thought I would be. It seemed as though the closer it came the sicker, I got. At one point, I was taken to the nurse's office for having dizzy spells. The weekend before spring break, I felt worst of all. It was Saturday night, and all of my friends were going to a party that the Kappa's were having.

"You goin', Jeffrey?" Henry asked as he poked his head in my room. "No, man, I feel terrible. I'll see y'all later."

My first intention was to go to my room and sleep. But, before I could change into my nightclothes, a female friend came by. She was a freshman I had spent a lot of time with recently and was considering establishing a serious relationship with. Her name was Candace, Candy for short.

She asked me to go downstairs with her to the lobby to watch TV. I agreed to in spite of my not feeling well. We stayed downstairs for several hours, playing cards and watching videos on MTV. I was enjoying myself and for a while I forgot about my sickness. That was, until around three o'clock a.m.

At that time my sickness got worse. I suddenly had a migraine headache, and the lower part of my stomach began to hurt. It hurt so badly that I could no longer play it off. As a result, I stood up grabbing my mid-section, kneeled over across the small card table and told Candy and the other students who joined us in our card game that I had to go to my room.

Without completely explaining what I felt, I ran upstairs to my room. I then fell asleep only to be awakened by somebody knocking on my door.

"Jeffrey. Jeffrey Thomas, the telephone is for you."

"The telephone, this early?" I said. Who in the world could it be?

I had this uneasy feeling about answering this call. I took my time getting to it.

When I did answer, it was Jake's voice that I heard. "Hello, Jeffrey. How are you doin'?" he asked.

He then went on asking me how things were going in Augusta, and if I had a girlfriend yet. I answered Jake's questions, but I knew he was avoiding telling me something. I knew he had something on his mind.

"What's wrong, man?" I asked him. "I know you didn't call me this early to ask me that."

"Well," he said, "I really hate to tell you this, but, well, Hank was killed."

Before I could say anything, a deep sharp pain traveled through my body. Tears automatically began to shower down my face. Lord, please don't let this be true. First Mookey, now Hank, both died in less than a year. It can't be. The phone was silent for moments before I regained my composure.

"What happened, Jake? Tell me."

"Well, it happened around three o'clock this mornin'. Hank was in the car with his cousin, and they had an accident. Three other people died in the accident. Hank's brother, Kevin, is in critical condition."

Jake went on to explain to me the details of what happened. He started by saying that at this moment Hank's parents don't know whether to plan a funeral for one or two. Jake's voice saddened with each word.

"Hank was in the passenger seat of his cousin's car. They were drag racing around Fall Creek Parkway while takin' the other passengers home. One of the other passengers who died was Verona."

Verona was an attractive sixteen year-old junior in high school. I had known her since she was seven. She lived around the corner from us and sometimes I'd cut her family's grass.

"Anyway, Jeffrey, Hank died on impact from what I was told." Jake and I talked about this for about an hour. I didn't want to hang up the phone, because then I knew I'd be alone. No one else here at Paine knew Hank, so they couldn't really sympathize with me.

It was discovered later that he died of a crushed pelvis. Even today, I wonder if the pain that I was feeling that Saturday was a premonition of Hank's death. I wonder too if the intense pain I felt that night was directed to me so that I could relieve him of some of the pain that he could have had. I hope so.

When I returned to my room I stayed there until dinner time. I explained what happened to Rev and my other friends. They knew that I was extremely hurt. I stayed in my room for the next three days. I didn't go to any of my classes. On the fourth day, I packed my things and headed for Indianapolis to attend my very best friend's funeral.

When I arrived home in Indianapolis, before I could open the door to our house, my mother and uncle greeted me with sympathetic expressions.

"I'm sorry about Hank," Momma said, as she led me into the house.

I wasn't home ten minutes before I received a call from Jake. Then other friends began to call. Bobby called to say that I was the first person he thought about upon hearing the news.

On the day of the funeral, I was in a dismal state. It was now that my best friend's death was really beginning to hit me. I don't remember saying two words all day, until the funeral. All of my friends from Broad Ripple were there. Many of them embraced me as if I had lost a brother. In actuality, I did lose a brother. I sat in the very back of the funeral home all by myself. All I thought about was Hank's big smile and his jovial demeanor.

Initially, I held back the tears, thinking I was too old to cry. Suddenly my pride escaped me, and my emotions came forth. Realizing that I would never see my best friend again, I continued to cry. I'll miss you, Hank.

When I returned to school, there were only a few more weeks left before the summer break. I managed to catch up in all my classes and finished the semester with average grades. I became homesick, and therefore, I knew that I wasn't going to summer school. I completed my first year of college, and for that, I was thankful. It's just unfortunate that I can't share my experiences with the same persons I shared them with before.

When I did get back to Indianapolis, I found that a lot of things had changed during that one year. Bobby was not just selling drugs, but he was using them too. I heard they really got him messed up too.

People were saying that he was borrowing money from everyone and taking things that didn't belong to him. I hated to hear this about a person like Bobby. He had great potential. I don't know where he went wrong. He had a mother and a father in the same home. He was an only child, so he was given more things than any of the rest of us. Not only that, he got good grades in high school. I can't figure out what his turning point was.

I was also told that Tuffy was still selling drugs, but unlike Bobby, he was not using them. Therefore, he was making a lot more money. I found that to be true when I saw Tuffy a few weeks after I'd arrived. He was at the car wash. He was driving a brand new Mercedes Benz. When he saw me, he rushed over to me and showed it off.

"What up, Jeffrey? Check out my new ride, man. Its sweet, isn't it? This is what's happenin', man. If you want to make it in this world, you have to get with the program. You sittin' around tryin' to go to college and do it the white man's way. Man, you'll never get somethin' like this," he told me as he pointed to his car. He then sped off in his just-washed, sparkling new car with his rap music blasting from the speakers.

I wasn't surprised to hear Tuffy say what he said. He always asked about me, and made crazy remarks like, "That fool wastin' his life" and "Is he still a Jesus freak?" I never felt the need to respond to his ridiculous comments, because I knew it would only lead to an extended and unnecessary debate. Tuffy was not the type of person to let you get the last word.

I had been home for about a month before I found a job. It was a minimum wage job, but it was the best I could find. While even being in college, it's hard for a young black male to get a good job. The job was at a recycling warehouse. I received bags of aluminum cans and newspapers from people, weighed them in, and gave them whatever money they earned. The best part about this job was that it gave me a lot of time to read my bible and be by myself.

I was the only one working there for the most part. There were two older white men employed there, too, but they spent most of the day elsewhere.

I was only making twenty-five dollars a day. Once Tuffy found out, he made it a point to tease me.

"Fool, what you in college for?" he'd sometimes say.

One day I was at a McDonald's with this new female friend I'd recently met at church. Tuffy and some of his friends came in a little while later.

"Hey, Jeffrey, I got some aluminum cans in my car. Go weigh 'em and give me my money," Tuffy said. He and his friends began to laugh.

Initially, I got angry by Tuffy's stupidity, but fortunately, it did not manifest itself.

I had already prayed about Tuffy and his problem. The word of God comforted me in times like these.

"But I tell you who hear me; Love your enemies, do good to those who hate you, bless those who curse you, pray for those who mistreat you." Luke 6:27,28 (NIV)

As that scripture came to me, so did a sigh of relief. I then was able to laugh with Tuffy and his friends. Before I left the restaurant, I walked over, shook Tuffy's hand and wished him well.

Working didn't give me too much time to spend with my friends, Ricky and Jake.

However, we did find some time late at night to hang out. We had to hang out at night because Jake had an evening job. He didn't get off work until around eleven o'clock. We'd usually all just get together and go to a park or to one of our homes and play games.

We met Sherri and Tracy, who soon began to join us in our late night adventures. Sherri and Tracy were two girls we met in high school. They, too, were Christians. Our relationships were strictly platonic, until Ricky and Tracy began to hit it off.

I spent more time with Ricky than anyone else in our group, because we both got off work around the same time. Ricky was the type of person who was very quiet. In fact, until he met us, he used to be by himself most of the time. I can recall him telling me that his mother was surprised at his new attitude.

"I remember when you used to always be home. Now, I hardly see you," he told me she said. I could tell that Ricky was really enjoying our friendship. He would always call me as soon as I got home from work. He called so much that he no longer had to leave his name, because my family knew his voice.

He would usually call to see if I wanted to play basketball at Tarkington Park. We loved to play basketball. Ricky was a much better player than I was. I can recall once, during the mile walk to the park to play ball, we noticed that we were going in the wrong direction.

"Hey, where are we goin', man?" I asked.

At that point, we both looked around and realized that we were walking over to Hank's house. It had only been three months since he died. Before then we would walk over there all the time. Hank only lived a couple of blocks from the park. Ricky and I had gotten so caught up in our conversation that we were just walking over to Hank's house without thinking.

A month later, Jake, Ricky, and I were supposed to go play ball at one of Jake's relative's houses out in the suburbs. Jake and I had been looking for Ricky all day, but we couldn't find him anywhere, until we called Tracy's house. He had been there all day. He said he'd be there a while longer.

"Go on without me," he said.

After Jake and I returned from playing ball, it was very late. Since it was Saturday, I decided to spend the night at Jake's. The next day, as I started to walk home, I decided to stop by Ricky's house first. Before I could get there, Jake's mother drove up.

"Where are you goin', Jeffrey? Do you need a ride?"

Since I was offered a ride, I decided to forego Ricky's house and go straight

home.

"Thanks for the ride," I told Jake's mom as I headed to my house. When I got

inside, my mother told me that some girl named Tracy had been calling me all day. Before Momma could continue, the phone rang.

"Jeffrey, telephone," Pat said from the bedroom.

As I was walking towards the phone, a strange, solemn feeling came over me.

When I got the phone, Tracy was on the other end.

"Jeffrey, did you hear what happened?" she said in a hurried, sorrowful voice. "No, I didn't. What happened?"

"Well," she said, "Ricky got killed."

My first reaction to this was that she was joking. In a minute, Ricky's going to pick up the phone and say that this is a joke. I waited momentarily.

"Tracy, why are you jokin' with me? You know how I feel about stuff like this."

"I'm not jokin', Jeffrey," she said. "Last night, while Ricky was walkin' home, he was hit by a drunk driver. He died this mornin' at Indiana University Hospital."

I still refused to believe this nonsense. There was no way Ricky could be dead when he knew I just lost Hank and Mookey. I can't believe Tracy would play with me like this. I then hung up the phone without saying goodbye. What I decided to do then was catch the bus down to 46th where Ricky lived in order to see what was going on.

As I sat on the bus, it felt like the longest ride ever. My mind was in a world of its own. I looked around the bus and saw people talking, but I couldn't hear them. It was like I was moving in slow motion.

When the bus arrived on 46th Street, I rushed off and ran down the street to Ricky's house. At this time the sun was going down and it began to rain. A strong wind then came from nowhere. This wind rushing against my back only added to my speed as I continued down the street. When I was walking up the stairs to his porch, I noticed that the door was open. As I walked to the screen door, I could see the silhouettes of several people inside. A huge lightning bolt flashed across the sky. Then, suddenly I heard people crying.

At that moment, reality struck me. I stood standing at the door in disbelief, wondering what my world was coming to, wishing and praying that this was just a dream, a dream, . . .

"Hey, Jeffrey! Jeffrey!" a voice called from the other side of the door. "Come in." It was Ricky's brother, Jesse.

I didn't have to ask if it was true once I got inside. The expression on each face answered my question. I felt unusually weak at this point. Therefore, I walked over to the sofa and sat down. I was in the living room by myself for several minutes alone, thinking, crying and asking God how this could have happened. Then Jesse walked in.

"Jeffrey, here are some of the last pictures we took," he said.

He gave me the pictures. I saw Ricky's face, smiling like he always did. I began to break down even more. This had to be the worst moment in my life.

"All of my friends are dyin'," I said.

When Jesse left the room, I left the house. I went back to my house only to find my family waiting there for me. I knew that they must have heard about what happened, because of the silence that greeted me.

"Are you doin' alright, son?" my mother asked. Those were the only words she said to me all day. In fact, those were the only words that anyone said to me. After all, what could they say?

When Mookey died they comforted me. When Hank died, they comforted me. Now here's Ricky; all in less than a year. What can they say? They could say nothing, absolutely nothing, and that's exactly what I wanted to hear.

I spent all day in the back room crying and praying. I felt like a seventy-year-old man whose friends were all dying of old age. I'm not seventy, though. I'm nineteen. I don't deserve this. I could see if I were still in a gang, and we were dying from doing something wrong, but that's not so. Why is this happening? Lord, give me strength.

I stayed home from work all week long until after the funeral. When I did return to work, my coworkers knew that I wasn't the same person. I explained to them how I felt, and they sympathized.

"You can go home if you want to," the boss said.

I refused the offer to go home. Instead, I stayed at work. As usual, I was left to work alone. The boss and his assistant went on about their usual daily duties.

The warehouse that I worked in was very big. The front of the building was not closed in. There was no wall to keep the weather out. The wind and the heavy rains made the place particularly cold that day. Being alone at work was commonplace, but today, I was lonely. My heart was heavy.

I've lost my friends. Death. Death. Why do people have to die? I have never thought about death so intensely. I felt that death could not be so bad since my nice friends lost their lives. The more I pondered on this matter the more depressed I became. I sat in front of the large conveyor belt, as old newspapers traveled up onto the big trailer truck where they were dumped and thought about death.

I was at the lowest point in life. All of a sudden, a piece of newspaper flew off of the conveyor belt and landed on my lap. I picked the paper up and unfolded it. I then realized that it was a religious article from some Christian newspaper. This seemed unreal, scary even. The article read,

"He will wipe every tear from their eyes. There will be no more mourning or crying or pain, for the old order of things has passed away. He who was seated on the throne said, "I am making everything new!" Then he said, "Write this down, for these words are trustworthy and true." He said to me, "It is done. I am the Alpha and the Omega, the Beginning and the End. To him who is thirsty I will give to drink without cost from the spring of the water of life. He who overcomes will inherit all this, and I will be his God and he will be my son." Revelations 21:48 (NIV)

I must have read this three or four times. It was just what I needed to hear. I didn't question the reality of the paper landing on my lap, for I already knew that God was alive. I then immediately got on my knees and began to pray.

As I prayed, I truly felt the Holy Spirit upon me. It was oh, so real, more real than it had ever been. I felt as though I was physically being lifted out of the chair and cuddled like a baby in the arms of the Lord. My belief, my faith in God has always been real, but never had I experienced this. The Holy Spirit was comforting me. My depression left me, and I became excited. I knew that beyond this life, there was joy, unspeakable joy. My excitement built up so strong that before I knew it, I started shouting, screaming, and speaking in tongues. I began to jump with happiness.

"Thank you, Jesus!" I shouted.

I heard my echo bounce off of the empty walls of the warehouse. I was the only one there, but I was not alone. Not anymore, I would never be alone again.

My joy lasted well beyond that day. I was a new creature.

I thought about that experience for days to come. There was a time in my life when I'd see people shouting and speaking in tongues at church, and I immediately began to think that they were faking, but not anymore. I know that it can be real. I know that the Spirit is real, and from now on, I was going to focus more on the life to come.

My attitude transcended into the next school year. I went back to Paine College, not with the attitude that I might fail, but that I will succeed. This time, not only will I succeed in my grades, but in my lifestyle as well.

I became more popular with the students. I started participating in the drama classes, subsequently, winning Best Actor and Best Comedian Awards the following three years. I was also elected to the Student Government Association and became very active in numerous other organizations. I came under the impression that no longer will I live life just to get by, but I will succeed. I will let my light shine.

"To know the love and peace, joy and power and comfort in your heart, Jesus said, is like having a great light inside you. Indeed, when people have this inner peace and joy, light seems to shine out of their faces and their eyes." Luke 11:33-34 (NIV)

And my light shined indeed. In May of 1989, I graduated from college with a BA Degree in Criminology Sociology. What a blessing! For someone who entered college through a whim, I did very well. Not only did I graduate but also during my collegiate years, I served as Vice President of the Student Government Association, President of the NAACP, and Editor in Chief of the college newspaper. I also won numerous awards for "Best Attitude" and "Humanitarian."

My mother made it to my graduation. I was glad to see her. My brother drove her there, June. He brought along his kids Erica,

Charles and Tommy, Jr. His wife, Doris, also came, along with my baby sister, Joyce.

CHAPTER SEVENTEEN
The Blueprint

My life is a testimony, not only to me, but to others as well. I knew that if I could change, anyone could. However, I felt that in order for a person to truly change their wicked ways they must be guided by the words of Jesus Christ. All other change is superficial. This was the philosophy that I subscribed to, and this is what I advocate.

After graduation, my desire to bring hope to the youths, particular black males, increased tremendously. Unfortunately, crime had increased as well. A new drug had also come on the scene. I had heard and read a lot about "crack" while studying, but I would not learn of its true effects until the summer of '89.

It was during this summer that I returned to Indianapolis to seek a career in youth development. Finding a job in this area was not as easy as I thought. Therefore, I found plenty of time to reunite with some of my friends. One such friend was Bobby. I knew that Bobby had joined Tuffy in selling drugs on the street corner. However, I felt that because Bobby and I had grown up together and that I knew that he respected me, maybe there was still a chance that I could still reach him.

Before I could begin my neighborhood search for Bobby, I was informed of some bad news. I was told that Bobby was in the hospital. He had gotten shot. He had stopped taking care of himself and began to live outside. Bobby started using more of the drugs than he was selling. As a result, he got himself in debt with the drug suppliers. He then began to rob and steal from people all kinds of people, including his friends.

One day Bobby broke into the home of one of his best friends, June bug. While leaving the house, Bobby was shot in the back by June bug. Now my grade school buddy was lying in Wishard Hospital with three bullet wounds to the back.

I went to visit him as soon as I heard the news. He was in critical condition, but the nurse allowed me in his room anyway. When I entered the room, I saw Bobby lying there motionless with tubes all in his body. I strolled over to him, held his hand, and began to pray. I prayed long and hard for my dear friend. I knew that he heard me, and I hoped that he would change.

To my dismay, this experience did not change Bobby. Less than two months after he was released from the hospital, he resumed selling drugs.

Tuffy had become one of the biggest drug dealers in Indianapolis. Now he had two Mercedes'. He also had two BMW's and one Bronco. I went to visit Tuffy one day to see this former friend, now King Pin, for myself. When I got to his apartment complex, he seemed happy to see me. He was in the parking lot washing one of his cars.

"What's up, Jeffrey?" he said. "You see all these vehicles I got, fool? Workin' for the white man won't get you this. I don't care how much schoolin' you got."

I explained to Tuffy that my purpose for being there was to try and talk some sense into his head before he got killed or locked up. He informed me that he wasn't worried about that because he had the best lawyer money could buy. As I stood there, another guy pulled up in a nice car.

"Hey, Tuffy! I'm starvin'. When you gonna feed me?" the guy yelled from the car. I guess that was some drug talk or something. Anyway, Tuffy motioned to the driver to come back later.

We must have talked for about an hour. Tuffy didn't conform to my way, but he did mention that once he got a million in cash, he would stop. Tuffy was very stubborn. I knew he wouldn't listen to me much longer. Therefore, I began to leave. Before I could, though, Tuffy yelled for me to come back.

"Jeffrey, did I tell you I was movin'? Yeah, I'm movin' into a house, a big house," he said.

"Where is this house?" I asked him.

"It's right here." Tuffy then reached into the back seat of his car and pulled out a blueprint. "it's being' built as we speak. I'll be movin' shortly," he said.

I was not impressed with the arrogance Tuffy displayed by being a drug dealer. I shook my head as if to say, Shame on you. Before leaving I turned and said, "Hey, Tuffy, I'm building' a house, too."

"Where's the blueprint?" he asked sarcastically.

I reached into my rear pocket and handed him my Bible.

"Here it is. I'm buildin' a house that no rain, wind, or tornado can destroy."

"But Christ is faithful as a son over God's house. And we are his house, if we hold on to our courage and hope of which we boast." Hebrews 3:6 (NIV)

"As you come to Him, the living stone rejected by men but chosen by God and precious to Him-you also, like living stones, are being built into a spiritual house to be a holy priesthood, offering spiritual sacrifices acceptable to God through Jesus Christ." I Peter 2:4 (NIV)

I saw Tuffy only two more times after that meeting. Four months had passed before I heard anything about him again. The news then was that Tuffy was in jail. I was told that he had gotten picked up at the airport with six kilos of cocaine. Due to the amount of drugs, he had, he was placed in a private cell to be turned over to the Federal Justice System upon arraignment. The newspaper later verified this information. I don't know if I'll ever see Tuffy again, but I pray that wherever he is, he takes hold to God's word and begins to do what he knows is right.

CHAPTER EIGHTEEN
A Vow to Keep

Since I had been home from college, I renewed my membership with the St. John Missionary Baptist Church. My participation in church activities, particularly with the youth, became known throughout the city. It was not long before Rev. Brown appointed me director of a new program that the church had started.

The St. John Youth Awareness Program was geared toward neighborhood youths, mainly young black males involved in gang or other criminal activities. I was blessed to have been appointed to such a position, and I vowed to do my best to produce results. I was so confident in my ability to produce change in our community that I chose to initiate this program by working with the so-called roughest neighborhood in the city of Indianapolis, the Brightwood community.

I had always known about Brightwood. As a child, I tried to keep away from that neighborhood because of its bad reputation. Today that reputation still stands. Now, though, I'm not afraid. Instead, I'm excited about the opportunity to make a change in the lives of a group of people who I was told couldn't be changed.

I met with one of the deacons at our church, Mr. Teddy Ray, and told him about my intentions. He was excited about what I wanted to do, and he promised to assist me whenever I needed him. Assist me was what he did too. Mr. Ray called me late one evening and mentioned to me that he was going to a high school the following day. This school, he said, was the high school that most of the youth from Brightwood attended.

He told me that this would be a great opportunity for me to speak to the troubled youth in an effort to establish a relationship. I gladly accepted.

The next day when we arrived at the high school, we went to the principal's office. Mr. Ray introduced me and told the principal about my intentions.

"That is great. We have a lot for you to work with here," the principal remarked.

He picked up a list of the names of the most troubled youths from the Brightwood community. And called them into the office. Once the youths arrived, we began to discuss problems and other issues that they faced in their community.

After about thirty minutes, the youths began to open up to me. They all talked about guns, drugs, robbery and a host of other things they saw happening in their community. I was told about how difficult it was to not be involved in these illegal activities when this is all they are faced with.

Even though these young guys tried to display a tough gangster demeanor, I felt compassion for them. I knew that inside, each of these young men was a charming normal young boy who just wanted to be given a chance. Many of these young black boys are expected to be bad, and, therefore, they are not given a chance. Neither in their schools nor in their neighborhoods were they given a chance. It was easy for me to relate to them, and I had a strong desire to bring a positive image in the lives of these young men.

As they continued to talk, I began to pray. I prayed to God that He'd give me something to say-- something that would enlighten and motivate these kids to at least begin to try to be different. At that time, I was given a thought.

"Okay, since you guys feel like you are given a raw deal in society, I want y'all to tell me what is it that y'all feel will help you with becoming productive students and simply better kids in general?"

One young man named "Big Mike" stood up.

"Well, what you doin' is goodcomin' to speak to us and stuff. But people always come around once or twice. If we had someone who would come around often an' talk to us an' treat us like normal people, we'd be alright."

I was pleased to hear that, because that's what I wanted the St. John Youth Awareness Program to be about.

"Well, fellas," I said, "that is what I'm here for. I want the opportunity to meet ya'll all of you. I know that God has given each one of you a specific talent. However, if you do not know Him, you won't know what your talent is." I then devised a schedule to meet with them every Tuesday. I told them that I would drive the church bus to their neighborhood to pick them up every Tuesday at six o'clock.

After the meeting with the kids, I met with Mr. Ray and Dr. Brown to discuss the specifics of this program. We decided, once we got permission from the parents, to allow the youths to meet at least once a week at the church. During those meetings, we would discuss neighborhood problems, and relate them to similar situations in the Bible and try to solve them with biblical solutions. I must admit I was uncomfortable at first about handling this type of responsibility. However, the discomfort didn't last long because I knew that what I would be doing was the will of God.

Before we started meeting with the kids at the church, I made sure that I was spiritually equipped. I prayed to God each day, as well as, read much literature on youth, crime and Christ. In my readings, I came to the conclusion that in order for these young people to change from bad to good, it is imperative that they include Christ. I absolutely and unequivocally feel that there is no other way. Many people would argue this by saying these young people don't really need Christ, but instead need jobs or more community centers. Well, I don't disagree that a job would help, but how many people have jobs and still no happiness or true joy?

I later worked in a prison for two years, and I found out that many of the inmates there had jobs at the time of their offenses. A job didn't stop them from committing a crime. It just changed the type of crime that they committed. For example, with a job, they may not rob anyone, but they still may kill someone in an argument or commit one of the other thousand offenses that don't involve money. A job may change the financial state, but having a Christian mind changes the mental state and the will to do wrong.

"Do not conform any longer to the pattern of this world but be transformed by the renewing of your mind." Romans 12:2 (NIV)

CHAPTER NINETEEN
Let's Serve

After obtaining the objectives of the St. John Youth Awareness Program, it was quickly introduced to the youth of the Brightwood community. Without hesitation, the program was adopted by the community and accepted by the youths. Glory to God! One of the reasons I feel the program was so easily accepted was that it received the blessing of our Lord and Savior. Another reason was that I and my fellow Christian brothers who assisted me with this project, Jake and Reggie, approached the youths in a humanistic way. We went to them proclaiming the necessity in having Christ in their lives, not proclaiming ourselves to be Christ.

In an article written about the St. John Program by the Indianapolis Recorder more than a year after the program's existence, a youth was quoted as saying, "We can relate to Jeffrey, Jake, and Reggie because they were once like us, and they changed."

Change was something I spoke of often. I informed them during our weekly meetings that change would happen inevitably. Change is something we can't control. How we change is something we can control. I advocated that they could either be changed by society or by the acceptance of Christ.

Not only was changing an issue, but the consequences of change as well. To give them a real visible reason to understand the consequences of change, we often took them on field trips to the local prisons and colleges. In the prisons they actually saw people who were once like them. Unfortunately, instead of accepting God's philosophy, many of them accepted the 'hood's philosophy, which is "Get all you can get, regardless of who it hurts."

Another reason that this program was successful was that we presented a comfortable environment to the youth members. We made them want to come to the meetings by supplying them on Tuesdays with food usually prepared by the women of the church. Then we kept them interested in hearing God's words by using current events.

We'd take a story out of the newspaper about something that happened in the 'hood about either someone who killed someone or someone who got killed for doing something wrong. Then we'd present to them the choices made by the individuals and the ultimate consequences. Most of the time, I'd try to put myself in the mind of the individual who was killed while doing wrong and take it step by step. With each step, I'd present to them what happened and what could have happened if the individual would have chosen Christ's way.

One such example was about a twenty-five year old man a person I happened to go to high school with. His name was Louis Brown.

Louis was an extremely quiet individual in high school. I can't ever remember him bothering anyone. He was always smiling. I remember Louis especially well because he had a big afro at a time when afros were not in style. I teased him often about this, but he never got upset. That is why I was shocked seven years later when I turned my TV to the news and found out that he was killed by the police during a robbery.

Many of the youth could relate to Louis' death, because it received above average media attention. In fact, his death sparked protest among local black community leaders. The reason for all the fuss was Louis was shot five times with a 9mm pistol.

The shooting was argued to be unnecessary because a weapon wasn't found on him. Not only that, but the officer who first arrived on the scene initially radioed headquarters that the suspect had been apprehended. A minute later, this same officer radioed headquarters again and said the suspect was dead.

For about two months after this incident, city leaders met at the city council building in protest. I, too, joined in that protest. I was furious. This was a blatant act of a police officer using much more than minimal force to apprehend a suspect: pure police brutality.

Police brutality, though, was not what I discussed with the youth at the church. Instead of focusing on the officer's actions, we focused on Louis' actions. What would make a clearly sane well-liked high school graduate like him commit a crime of this magnitude? He had a decent job, and he never got in trouble with the law before. Could it be that he was just tired of having just enough money or, was he just fed up with abiding by the laws of society and just decided to see what it was like on the other side? I can't tell you exactly what was going on in the mind of this young man. However, I have done research and followed up on a lot of information concerning this case.

Therefore, I'd like to hypothetically put myself in Louis' shoes for a while.

It was assumed that he knew the person he was robbing. He knew that this individual brought money out of the store at midnight. He knew that police did not heavily surround the area where the crime would take place. He also knew that he'd be driving a sports car and could get away quickly. Finally, he knew he wanted the money. Now a situation like this appeared to be an easy target, a sure deal, tempting, even to this young man, who had never committed a crime before.

The scenario that my brother Louis found himself in reminds me of the situation that Eve found herself in while in the Garden of Eden (Genesis 3). Eve found herself tempted. But you see Eve was not tempted initially. When she first saw the tree, there was no desire to eat that fruit, because there were plenty of other fruits to eat there. Her temptation developed as a result of Satan telling her that nothing would happen to her if she ate from this tree. She knew it was wrong and against God, but Satan made it desirable to her. He conned her into believing that there was nothing to lose.

I feel Louis, too, found himself in the Garden of Eden the day he robbed this store. I can see it now, Satan telling him," For all this time you've done well. You did what the law expects you to do. But, look at you now. You don't have any money. Well, let me tell you, Louis, I know how your problems can be over. You remember that store on 56th Street? Well, you know that the manager takes the money from the store at twelve o'clock every night. You also know that on an average day, they make possibly over two thousand dollars. Imagine that, Louis, two thousand dollars in your pocket. It'll take you at least two months to make that, my brother."

Satan also continued to tell him about the neighborhood being absent of police and about his sports car being able to quickly flee the scene. However, there was one thing that Satan didn't tell poor Louis. It was the same thing he didn't tell Eve. That was, if you disobey God,

" . . . You shall surely die." Genesis 2:17 (NIV)

God didn't say you might die, or you could possibly die. He said you'd surely die. And die is unfortunately what my brother, Louis, did.

When I explained this to the young gang members, I focused on the bad, evil choices that people make. I concluded by telling them that the first thing wrong that Eve and Louis did was entertain Satan's conversation.

"If you focus more on God, who is the Creator of both heaven and earth, the King of Kings, then you will not have the desire to entertain any of Satan's evil suggestions," I told them.

In Matthew 9:3 (NIV), Jesus is quoted as saying, "Why do you entertain evil thoughts in your hearts?" Entertaining Satan's thoughts produces the desires to do Satan's work.

"Then, after desire has conceived, it gives birth to sin; and sin when it is full grown gives birth to death." James 1:15 (NIV)

"Blessed is the man who perseveres under trial, because when he has stood the test, he will receive the crown of life that God has promised to those who love him." James 1:12 (NIV)

CHAPTER TWENTY
Decisions

It was that type of ministering that made our program a success. In fact, the program was only four months old before the local media found out about it. I was contacted by a couple of newspapers and television stations. They asked me if I would allow them to sit in on a meeting and interview me. I denied their request, because I didn't want the media to interview me. The program wasn't about me. It was about the youth of the Brightwood Community. Therefore, I felt that it was they who should be interviewed. However, I also felt that this wasn't the right time for that interview. I then asked the reporters to come back after the program was at least a year old. That way the youth themselves would be able to answer any questions themselves.

When that time came, the reporters were invited back. They interviewed the youth and sat in on one of our meetings. Many of the youth were raising their hands to speak, unlike before. They talked about how the program influenced their lives. When asked by a reporter from the Indianapolis Star if any of them were ever involved in gangs, all of them raised their hands. An article was written in the October 19, 1990, issue entitled "Brightwood Gang Strives to Make It."

One of the main words that I make sure to mention each meeting is DECISIONS. Good decisions. It is my prayer that after our meetings each student will be able to concentrate more on the decisions they make. You see, most programs that I have been involved with deal with what I believe to be the surface issues, such as drugs, gangs, sex, school dropout and the like. These issues, although they are important and need to be addressed, are not the root issues. The root is the decision to get involved in the gangs, drugs, sex, etc.

For example, King David saw beautiful Bathsheba, Uriah's wife, bathing on the roof. He then made a conscious decision to pursue her. As a result, surface issues arose: adultery took place, even murder, as well as the birth (and untimely death) of an illegitimate child. (2 Samuel 11).

"But each one is tempted when by his own evil desire, he is dragged away and enticed. Then, after desire has conceived, it gives birth sin, and sin when it is conceived gives birth to death. Don't be deceived, my dear brothers." James 1:14-16

CHAPTER TWENTY-ONE
Godly Intentions

As a result of all of the media attention focused on the St. John Youth Awareness Program, many people started coming to the church to sit in on meetings. At one point the number of people coming by was becoming a nuisance. Therefore, we asked that each person contact the church to make an appointment before just popping up in our meetings. I didn't mind people coming by, if their intentions were good.

College students came by because they were doing reports on various types of programs. I can respect that. People from other youth programs came by because they wanted to know what was making this program successful. Each time I was faced with that question I'd always say the same thing.

"Our program is a success because we not only have good intentions, but godly intentions. A program without godly intentions cannot be a totally effective program. Without godly intentions, I'm convinced we couldn't produce these types of results; and no one can argue with results."

Dr. Tony Evans, in his book America's Only Hope states, "If we attempt to solve a problem without understanding the spiritual cause, and then thereby finding a spiritual solution, we cannot achieve a long term solution."

Not everyone's intentions were good. One day this popular politician came by. I was very glad to see him, and it was good to know that someone of his caliber had an interest in this type of program. Once he began to speak to me about why he was there, my interest in him turned into disappointment. He looked around and asked if any media was present. I told him no. He then stated that he had to leave.

Before leaving, he said, "Let me know when the media is coming back here.

Then I will come back to volunteer with the program."

This was a very disappointing statement to me. I felt that if he was sincere about working with our youth, the media shouldn't have to be there.

Working with the youth made me a more spiritual person, although, there were times when things didn't go my way. Several times when I went to pick up the kids in the church van, I'd find chaos in the neighborhood. There were times when I'd get there and see kids fighting in the streets or police officers handcuffing some of the youths. Once, I saw one of the kids selling drugs to an older boy. All of these incidents filled me with sorrow. At times, I'd wonder why I kept trying to help. I'd feel useless. Regardless of the negative experiences that I had, I couldn't see myself giving up. Something must be done.

Even though these kids are from a low income area, and have had run ins with the police, there is still hope for them. I felt that if I sat there idly and did nothing to try to better our youth, then I, too, am to blame. Because I know through personal experience that, "Troubled Kids Need Jesus Too."

ABOUT THE AUTHOR

Taken *Atlanta Journal Constitution, Gwinnett County* Section, Saturday December 17, 2005 Laughs are not what comic is focused on Veal hopes to change the lives of at-risk kids - Lateef Mungin - Staff

Lilburn comic Larry Veal hasn't been nearly as funny lately.

In front of crowds of Gwinnett school kids, Veal talks about crimes committed by wayward youth. Despite his tough subject matter, Veal gets his audiences to laugh and learn through his speeches. And through his nationally acclaimed program, "B-Moe Positive," he has changed the lives of countless at-risk kids.

Veal has been asked many times to talk to Gwinnett school students and counselors. Ten years into growing his youth mentorship program, Veal said it is hard to believe what his program has accomplished.

Veal estimates that he spoke to more than 100,000 students just last year in auditorium settings. About 110 youths also went through his 12-week program in small groups last year, Veal said.

It all started with an effort to answer the questions: Why do some youth commit crimes, and what can be done to stop them before they do it?

"His talks are wonderful," said Tikitia Glover, a counselor at Brookwood High School. "The students said they could really relate to him. They said he was real."

For Veal, the idea for his program came from real-life experience.

Back in 1995, while he was working as a metro Atlanta probation officer, his younger brother received a life sentence for an Indiana drug conviction.

About the same time, a 15-year-old boy in Veal's probation caseload was killed in a gun fight.

Then Veal learned that another of his probationers tried to use him as an alibi. When Veal told detectives the truth, the young man tried to enlist friends to kill him.

Veal said all those events showed him in graphic detail that he needed to do more for troubled youth than he could do as a probation officer. And that revelation ended his seven-year career as a probation officer.

"All the schools and courts were interested in was punishing kids for what they had done," said Veal. "I was more interested in finding out why they did bad things. And finding ways to prevent it."

Veal said he interviewed numerous kids and found that three factors contributed to most delinquent behavior: emotional issues, impulsive behavior and peer pressure.

Veal then created a curriculum that addressed those three issues and then took his program to churches, juvenile halls and schools. Veal also blended his brand of clean comedy into his presentations to keep his audiences' attention.

"It is an excellent program," said Tonya Criswell, who worked with Veal several years ago at a DeKalb County group home.

"I had nine boys in the home, ages 7 to 17, that he came in and consoled," she said. "And I could see a significant difference in the boys from the very first session."

One of the teenagers Veal is working with is 16-year-old Tuson Green of Snellville. Green's mother thought the youngster was on the verge of following his older brother into a life of crime. She heard about Veal's program and called him. That was three years ago.

"It definitely helped me when I was going through stuff to talk to Larry," Green said. "I had failed eighth grade before I worked with Larry."

Since that time, Green said, his life has turned around.

"Now I have not failed any grades," he said. "I've changed my relationship with my parents. And my goal is to be a Marine."

This type of a praise and work is a far cry from the days when Veal used to tell jokes to adult crowds at smoke-filled comedy clubs. Veal was featured on BET's "Comic View" and says he opened for the likes of Luther Vandross, Anita Baker and well-known funny men Chris Tucker and Cedric the Entertainer.

"I could have just stayed with comedy and had a level of success," Veal said. "But many things in my life told me I had to do something for the kids."

Made in the USA
Columbia, SC
27 January 2022